Forex and Cryptocurrency

The Ultimate Guide to Trading Forex and Cryptos. How to Make Money Online By Trading Forex and Cryptos in 2020.

David Uchiha

TABLE OF CONTENTS

INTRODUCTION

Welcome to *Forex and Cryptocurrency The Ultimate Guide to Trading Forex and Cryptos. How to Make Money Online By Trading Forex and Cryptos in 2020*. If you are reading this, you will find a trove of information that will help you to make sound investment decisions in the world of FOREX and cryptocurrencies.

This book is intended for all newcomers to both the world of FOREX and cryptos. We will be discussing the fundamentals of both of these markets in great detail. The main objective is to provide you with an education in this subject so that you can make sound investment decisions leading you to maximize your profits and obtain the best possible returns for your investment dollars.

Unlike the stock market, the FOREX and cryptos markets are open 24 hours a day. This means that you can trade any time you wish. This opens up a number of interesting possibilities as you can invest in both FOREX and cryptos without having to quit your day job or significantly alter your regular routine. In fact, all you need to do is make sure that you have the right setup to get started.

That's why we're here... we're here because we want to give you a head start that we wish we could have had when starting out investing. You see, most investors become successful through trial and error. Many times, you have to lose a great deal of money before you can become rich. Unfortunately, some investors lose their shirts before they can make serious money.

That doesn't have to be your case. With the education you will get in this book, you'll be able to make money without having to lose your shirt in the process. If anything, you'll have to become a student of these markets. After all, all successful investors dedicate time and attention to the study of their chosen market. Such investors strive to learn as much as they can. In doing so, they are able to maximize their returns without having to sacrifice their capital in the process.

If you are brand new to investing, don't worry. We have you covered. You don't need an advanced degree in finance to cash in on the markets. All you need is the willingness to put in the time and effort needed to learn the way the FOREX and crypto markets work. Once you get started, you'll see that these markets are not quite as complex as you might have thought. Sure, they do have their intricacies. But then again, with the education you can expect here, you won't be second-guessing.

So, let's get started on the journey that will lead you to become financially independent. At the end of the day, that's what all great investors seek. They are all after making as much money as they can so that their families are provided for. In addition, making money isn't so much a question of greed; it's a question of earning enough money to ensure security. This kind of security comes by way of financial independence.

Let's get on with it!

CHAPTER 1

Introduction To Forex And Cryptocurrency Trading

FOREX and cryptocurrencies (also known as "cryptos") are financial markets in which investors come together to make deals for the purpose of earning a profit. This is important to note as investors are not in it to lose money. They are in it to make as much money as possible. Naturally, there are winners and losers. Nevertheless, all investors try to be on the winning end as much as possible.

On the whole, most folks tend to become confused by the various types of financial markets. For instance, stocks are an entirely different market. There are also bonds, commodities, and derivatives. All of these markets have their characteristics. If you are keen on learning about them, by all means, take the time to do the research you need.

As for the FOREX market, you will find that it is the most dynamic of all financial markets. The reason for this is that FOREX is the most liquid market in the world. Since you are essentially trading currency, you are swapping money for money. This is something that you can do right from the comfort of your home. Best of all, FOREX is a 24-hour market as you are trading currency from all over the world. In short, you can trade anytime and anywhere.

This is why FOREX is so attractive to investors around the world.

However, FOREX is not for the faint of heart. FOREX requires you to pay close attention to the dynamics of the market itself. This means that you need to study what's happening so that you can be ready for any changes which may emerge. You can profit greatly from these changes, or you can sustain significant losses. It's all in the way you manage the situation unfolding around you.

Types of FOREX Markets

Considering that the FOREX market is essentially a marketplace in which currency is bought and sold, it behaves just like any other market. This implies that the great equalizer of the FOREX market is price. The difference here lies in the fact that price does not reflect the valuation of a commodity such as a car, a house, or a pair of jeans. In this case, price is the reflection of the valuation of one currency versus another. What this means is that you understand the value of one currency as it is expressed in terms of another.

The same situation occurs with any other commodity on the planet. The difference lies in the fact that it's easier to grasp the concept of a pair of jeans costing X amount of dollars as opposed to one Euro costing X amount of dollars.

With that in mind, FOREX is all about finding the mechanisms in which you can take one sum of money, exchanging it for another, and then exchanging that currency back into the original currency, for a profit, of course. This is the basic mechanism that you can use to conduct FOREX trades.

Just like other financial markets, there are several types of markets within the FOREX domain. So, we're going to be taking a look at what they are their characteristics.

The Spot Market

This type of market receives its name as it deals with the trade of currency at current prices. The current price of a currency is reflected by its exchange rate. In essence, an exchange rate is the ratio of one currency in terms of another.

When you travel, you commonly see exchange rates at airports. For instance, if you exchange US Dollars into Mexican Pesos, you might find that you'll get twenty-some Pesos for one US Dollar. This is an exchange rate. It is the price that a person is willing to pay or receive for another currency.

Also, you'll find the term "cross rates." While exchange and cross rates tend to be used synonymously, the difference lies in that exchange rates are used for the purpose of converting currency. The term cross rate is generally used as a reference regarding the valuation of one currency in terms of another. Additionally, you'll also find that leading currencies are "quoted" in terms of various currencies. This serves as a reference for investors who deal in international business.

As such, the spot market is where you buy and sell currency at current market prices. Market prices are set by supply and demand. These market forces converge as holders of currency look to sell while buyers look to find supply. In a perfect equilibrium, that is, there is a balance between buyers and sellers, price tends to be stable. This means that there is very little shift in price, if any. When there is an imbalance in market forces, the price tends to fluctuate accordingly. Generally speaking, when there is a greater supply, price tends to fall. When there is a greater demand, price tends to rise.

However, these market forces are immutable and may be subject to changes depending on the overall conditions of the market itself.

The most straightforward way to make money on FOREX is to buy low and sell high. However, this isn't always the case. In FOREX, there are times when you can make money by falling price. It all depends on what your objectives are.

The Futures Market

Since price (exchange rates) are set by market forces, you are subject to the fluctuations in price. This means that there is nothing you can really do to prevent prices from moving, or to influence them in the direction you wish. Unless you hold a vast investment capital, or if your influence is great on investor psyche, then you are basically at the mercy of market forces.

Often, both businessmen and investors look to reduce their exposure to this type of risk by engaging in the futures market. As its name suggests, you are making deals for the future. As such, this implies that you make a deal today with hopes of reducing your exposure to risk in the future.

For instance, you wish to purchase Swiss Francs in a month's time. However, you are concerned about the exchange rate down the road. So, you can take out a futures contract so that you lock in today's exchange rate on a deal that will happen in a month's time. Your counterpart will engage in the deal while also charging you a commission for their trouble. Often, the commission (also known as a "premium") you pay for the contract itself is far less than the difference you might have to pay if you don't take out the contract.

Some contracts stipulate that you don't have to execute the deal if you don't want to. In this case, you have an option to go through with the contract or not. If you choose not to go through with the deal, then all you lose is the premium you paid for the issuance of the contract.

As for international business, taking out these types of contracts makes a great deal of sense as it allows them to get a handle on their costs. This enables companies to reduce the risk of having raw materials, supplies, or merchandise skyrocket unexpectedly due to fluctuations in exchange rates. Also, it secures them funds that they can use to make payments. As a result, the futures market is a very active market in which you can engage if you choose to do so.

The Forward Market

On the whole, the forward market is the same as the futures market. The forward market is characterized by locking in current prices for a future deal. The difference lies in that the entire set of conditions surrounding these contracts are completely customizable. As a result, you can configure them to suit your individual needs and conditions.

In the forward market, it's common to find "options contracts." These contracts contain the various conditions which we have already described with the particular difference that they give holders an option to buy, or sell, depending on the specific terms of the deal. This implies that if holders are not keen on enacting the contract itself, they can choose not to go through with it. In the end, they only lose the underwriting fee charge for the contract.

The forward market can be a good source of deals for you. So, do look into it should you be interested in making the most of the potential deals in this type of market. Ultimately, you will have the choice to go through with the contract if it is best for you at that specific point in time.

Forex and Cryptocurrency

For most folks, understanding what cryptocurrency is can be challenging. On the whole, a crypto functions just like a regular currency. However, the difference lies in that crypto is a fully digital currency. This means that it will never have any physical issuance, as is the case of regular government-issued currencies.

In this case, cryptos are used in a digital sphere meaning that they are used solely within digital transactions. This implies that you would never be able to use crypto in a cash transaction, as is the case many times. For example, you could barter the sale of an item at a garage sale. But the payment for the item would happen digitally. As such, no cash would exchange hands.

Beyond that main difference, cryptos trade exactly the same way as a regular currency would. This is why investors are keen on cryptos as they function much the same way money does. Additionally, they can also be traded in the same manner that regular currencies are traded.

The reason why cryptocurrencies were born is due to the slowness that governments have had in reacting to the increasing presence of the digital world. Since there is a great deal of business taking place digitally, digital platforms and payment systems are needed.

However, it's not always easy to transition from regular hard currencies to a digital system. This implies a need for banks to adapt their practices to suit the needs of online business.

To solve this, cryptocurrencies emerged. In addition, cryptocurrencies are meant to be used as a means of avoiding the traditional banking system. While the intent is not to circumvent traditional banking for the purpose of illegal activity (though cryptos are the currency of choice for criminal groups), the fact of the matter is that using cryptos facilitates a great deal of transactions.

In fact, one of the core tents of cryptos is to facilitate transparency. Given the social nature of cryptos, users are put into a position in which they must ensure transparency at various turns. This is due to the shared ledger technology of the blockchain. In addition, transactions can't be simply erased from the system. Since there are multiple entries at various points in the system, erasing a transaction is impossible. This means that all transactions conducted in a specific cryptocurrency are recorded forever. This fosters transparency at all turns.

Top Cryptocurrencies

When talking about cryptos, it's safe to assume that the top one that comes to mind is Bitcoin. Since Bitcoin arrived on the scene in 2009, it exploded in popularity until it became the most-traded asset in recent history. In fact, the craze for Bitcoin got to be so big that it soared to over $20,000 per coin. If only individual stocks or commodities could reach these heights.

The reason why Bitcoin reached this price point is due to its relative scarcity. You see, Bitcoin is quite hard to produce. Given the nature of the blockchain and the computing power it takes to solve the math problems behind each transaction, individual Bitcoins have become quite hard to produce. Since there is a finite supply of Bitcoins, investors and speculators decided to get in on the action.

However, like all financial assets, the market could only take so much.

Eventually, Bitcoin's market valuation fell from $20,000 a coin to about $3,000 before rebounding to about $10,000. These wild swings are relatively common with newer assets, particularly when investors flock to enter the market on the fear of missing out. And while there has been talk of market manipulation, the fact remains that Bitcoin is the leader in the crypto space by far.

But it should also be noted that Bitcoin is not the only show in town. There are hundreds of other cryptos out there. Most of them don't sell for very much. In fact, you can get some for a little as pennies on the Dollar. Then, there are others which trade for considerably more.

Here is a list of the top 10 cryptos on the market today based on the market cap.

1. Bitcoin (BTC) $128bn
2. Ethereum (ETH) $19.4bn

3. XRP (XRP) $8.22bn

4. Tether (USDT) $6.4bn

5. Bitcoin Cash (BCH) $4.1bn

6. Bitcoin SV (BSV) $3.4bn

7. Litecoin (LTC) $2.6bn

8. EOS (EOS) $2.4bn

9. Binance Coin (BNB) $2.4bn

10. Tezos (XTZ) $1.5bn

There are some familiar names on this list, and some not-so. This list includes major players like Bitcoin, Ethereum, and Litecoin. Some not-so-familiar names include XRP and Tezos. Nevertheless, these coins have a considerable market cap. These are the market values estimated for the total amount of coins in existence for each crypto multiplied by their value per coin.

As you can see, there is a considerable amount of money in play within the crypto market. In total, there are 5,392 total cryptocurrencies (as of April 2020) with a total market value of $201bn.

That's a nice chunk of change.

What's more, cryptos are traded just like any other currency on the market today. This means that you have the unique opportunity to take part in a $200-billion market. Hence, there is a lot of money to be made by savvy investors.

One more thing: technology is the future now as it has always been. Therefore, the use of cryptos for everyday use will soon become a reality. That's why it's best to get in on the ground floor now, build up your portfolio and move on from there. You will surely find that the value there is to be made in this market will entice you to dig deeper into the possibility of investing and making a healthy profit.

Basic Forex Terminology

Like any other discipline, FOREX has a set of specialized vocabulary which you need to become familiar with. So, here are the main terms which you will find throughout this book.

Cryptocurrency. A digital currency that has many of the same functions as a regular fiat-based currency. It is digital in nature and contains specific encryption mechanisms that are used to regulate its issuance and use. These methods are used to verify the transfer of funds and operate independently of any country's jurisdiction. They are backed by the confidence of users and can be found on specific platforms created for their use.

Currency. The official government-issued means of payment which enables users to buy and sell goods and services. Currency acts as money as it is a store of wealth and allows for the measurement of the value of goods. It is also a means of settling accounts while also enabling individuals to transact across countries. Currency is issued by a central bank and backed by the financial position of a government.

Exchange rate. The expression of the value of one currency in terms of another. Exchange rates are the ratio in which one currency can be converted into another. For the purpose of international business transactions, various currencies may be used. Therefore, an exchange rate serves to create a means of establishing parameters of comparison among various currencies. Exchange rates also serve as a pricing mechanism in which foreign exchange markets can price one currency in relation to another.

FOREX. This is the "foreign exchange" market. It is the marketplace in which buyers and sellers of currency meet. Nowadays, it is a digital marketplace where transactions occur over the internet. Payments and accounts are settled electronically. The physical location of the FOREX market is the New York Stock Exchange in New York. However, virtually all of the transactions on the FOREX market happen over a digital platform. Investors who gain access to this platform can conduct trades without the need to be physically present at the stock exchange.

Leverage. This refers to the amount of funds needed to place a trade. In a manner of speaking, leverage means that you can place trades whose value is greater than the amount of funds you have deposited in your account. When you are required to have full backing, you cannot place a trade beyond the amount of money you have deposited in your account. However, if you are not required to have any amount of money deposited, you essentially have 100% leveraging. At 50% leverage, you can place a $100 trade with $50 deposited in your account.

Margin. Margin refers to the difference between the money you have deposited in your account and the value of your trade. If you place a trade using leverage, you will earn a margin when you make a profit. If you lose money on the trade, then you need to cover that margin. In such cases, you may get a "margin call." This means that the brokerage firm you are working with will ask you to pay the difference for the loss you have incurred. If your account has sufficient funds, the fund will simply be deducted.

PIP. "Price in points" or, pip, is the individual measure for the profit or loss in FOREX. Generally speaking, pips refer to percentage points on a trade. Pips are relative to the specific cross rates of two currencies. This means that if you have a 1:1 cross rate, pips will represent a much higher value than if you had a 1:100 cross rate.

Profit/loss. Simply put, this the money you make, or lose, on each trade. In FOREX, the stop-loss point refers to the point where you cut your losses, and the take-profit point alludes to the point in which you will exit a trade with the profit you have indicated.

Resistance level. This is the highest point in a data series, meaning the highest price point that a currency pair will hit before coming back down. The "resistance" is created as the price does not move beyond this point. When price pushes past a resistance level, the term "breakout" is used to refer to this situation.

Spread. Spread is the difference between your stop-loss and take-profit points. Essentially, you measure the difference between the amount of money you expect to make and the largest loss you are prepared to take.

Support level. This level refers to the lowest price point in a data set. This point serves as "support" as the price does not move below it. The main reason for this is that investors jump in to purchase at this point, thereby raising the price back up to the eventual resistance level. When prices fall through the support level, this is referred to as a "breakthrough."

CHAPTER 2

Fundamentals Of Cryptocurrency And The Blockchain

It seems that "cryptocurrency" and the "blockchain" have become buzzwords in recent years. Anyone who is looking into becoming an investor seems to be interested in getting a piece of the action. Since you are reading this book, it's fair to say you too, are interested in getting a piece of the action. As such, we will be looking at the fundamentals of cryptocurrency and the blockchain so that you can gain a much better perspective on this matter. In addition, we'll be discussing the overall functioning of this technology and what it means to the average individual.

It should be noted that the concept of cryptocurrency was born out of the need to have a means of payment that could go outside of the usual government-controlled systems. The idea was to create a safe and secure means of creating transactions in such a way that users could be certain that each transaction is fully secured.

This is important to note as most transactions, digital or otherwise, don't always have a secure platform. In fact, regular transactions lend themselves to fraud and illegal activity. In particular, cash economies create vast underground networks that criminals can exploit. Thoughts of drug dealers exchanging suitcases full of cash come to mind.

Consequently, cryptos are meant to work outside of usual central bank control while ensuring full transparency for all users. Nevertheless, critics of cryptos have pointed to the fact that criminals use cryptos to engage in financial transactions as these digital currencies work outside of networks supervised by law enforcement agencies.

This is true of lesser-known crypto. As a matter of fact, some cryptos have been created for this specific purpose. But when you deal with "official" cryptos, that is digital currencies that are fully transparent by the entire internet, so to speak, you know you have the assurance that you are not dealing with criminals. Rather, you are dealing with other folks who want a secure means of conducting business.

What Is the Blockchain?

When digital currencies first arrived on the scene, the concept of blockchain was born. Since then, this term has been replaced with the term "digital ledger." The reason for this name is that the blockchain is exactly that, a digital ledger.

If we consider traditional accounting principles, double-entry bookkeeping has a party and a counterparty in every register. Therefore, the blockchain uses this system to keep track of transactions. However, it takes this concept one step further by adding a third party who is in charge of verifying every transaction. In a manner of speaking, it's like having two friends agree on a bet and then having a third friend witness the agreement.

In this exact manner, the blockchain is able to ensure that every transaction is fully transparent. In order to conduct a transaction, both parties must be registered and verified users. This means that there are no anonymous individuals who can pretend to be someone else. If you are not verified, you cannot deal with official cryptos.

Furthermore, the third party, which certifies the transaction, must also be duly verified. This is what gives credence to the verification process. Once the transaction has been completed and verified, it is registered on multiple servers throughout the world. Thus, there is no centralization of data. If a user wished to erase a transaction, they would have to erase all servers on which the transaction was recorded. This is virtually impossible, as knowing the exact number of servers is quite difficult. Plus, all data can be quickly copied on to additional serves. As such, anyone wishing to erase transactions would need to shut the entire internet down, scour every possible server for records, and then delete them.

But then again, anyone with a copy on a hard drive that is not connected to the internet could simply upload them again.

Do you see why this system ensures full transparency?

The Verification Process

This is where the blockchain gets a bit tricky.

When a transaction between two parties takes place, it is not official until it has been verified by a third party. Once the third party has gotten on the blockchain to verify the process, the transaction is finalized, and the seller receives payment.

The way the verification process works is through the solution of a math problem. The third party that verifies the transaction must successfully solve a mathematical problem in order to successfully authenticate the deal. However, for this process to truly work, each problem has to be unique. Once a specific problem has been solved, it can never be used again. For instance, $2+2 = 4$ can only be used once. Upon its solution, it is registered so it can never be used again.

Given this specific characteristic, the blockchain needs to generate more and more problems in order to satisfy the amount of transactions. In theory, there is an infinite number of math problems to be solved. Consequently, there is potential for an unlimited number of transactions. Nevertheless, as transactions go, the difficulty of problems increases.

Now, it should be noted that these problems are not solved by hand; that is, the problem isn't solved by a person working with pen and paper. A computer would do that for them. The issue here is that the complexity of math problems consumes a certain amount of computing power.

This is where the challenge lies.

At first, the computing power needed to solve basic math problems was minuscule and could be completed in a matter of nanoseconds. However, the estimated amount of computing power needed to solve the blockchain's current problems is estimated to surpass the power of the average computer. Thus, an average computer needs several minutes to complete the verification problem. This is why the blockchain has slowed down in recent times.

By now, the blockchain is still functional. However, its future is rather unclear as there is no real way of predicting if it is sustainable indefinitely. Most experts agree that the blockchain is unsustainable as the amount of electricity that is required to run the verification process is quite large. Thus, other iterations of cryptos will eventually replace the blockchain with a much less energy-intensive system.

Coin Creation and Offering

At the outset of the blockchain, there wasn't a single coin in circulation. This meant that each coin had to be created by transactions that did not include a coin that was already in existence. Therefore, the two parties would make a deal, and after the verification process, they would be able to create a new coin.

The reason for this system was so that only the absolutely necessary number of coins would be created. This was purposely done to avoid the uncontrolled issuance of currency that governments engage in. As a result, only a set number of coins would be used to conduct a specific number of transactions.

Initially, it was thought that the blockchain could produce enough coins to run the entire world economy. However, experience has proven this to not be the case. There is a finite number of coins as the computing power and electricity needed to create them would eventually surpass humankind's ability. Thus, the only choice here would be to create a fixed number of coins.

The workaround to this situation was to create multiple cryptos in order to share the load, so to speak. Since then, a great deal of coins has been created. Some have quickly gained popularity, while others have remained within a niche market of users. For instance, gaming communities use very specific cryptos for in-app purchases or transactions during gameplay.

Other cryptos have taken the route that is known as an "initial coin offering" or ICO. An ICO is very similar to an IPO with a stock. In an ICO, the creator(s) of the crypto issues an initial number of coins which users can purchase at a specified market price. Like IPOs, underwriters determine the valuation of each coin based on its potential and possible utility. Some ICOs have been widely successful, while others have been a flop. Still, ICOs are generally met with the same expectation as IPOs, that is, the hope that an investor can get in early and clean up when the market begins to push up the price.

The History of the Blockchain

It might surprise you to find that the blockchain, at least the concept of it, dates back to the early 90s. Around that time, when the internet first began to emerge, so did the idea of a system in which computer networks could be used to conduct financial transactions. And so, the concept of the blockchain was born.

Since then, numerous attempts were made to bring this process to life. But it wasn't until computing power caught up to this idea that it became practical. That's why around 2008, Satoshi Nakamoto (pseudonym for the creator of Bitcoin) was able to make the blockchain operational. With the emergence of Bitcoin, literally, thousands of cryptos have come into existence. As such, we now have a myriad of coins to choose from.

But we need to go all the way back to 1991 to find that Stuart Haber and W Scott Stornetta first described the concept of what would become the blockchain. Their work revolutionized the information world though it was nothing more than a pipedream them.

In 1998, the first decentralized digital currency emerged as Nick Szabo began work on what was then known as "bit gold." The idea was to create the world's first digital currency, that is, a currency that wasn't controlled by a government or central bank.

A couple of years later, in 2000, Stefan Konst developed his theory on "cryptographic secured chains." These led to a set of guidelines on how they could be implemented for the purpose of ensuring that the idea of a decentralized currency could become a reality.

However, it wasn't until 2008 that developer(s) working under the guise of Satoshi Nakamoto published a white paper for the eventual model of what would become the blockchain as we know it today. It is unclear whether it was a single developer, or most likely a group of developers who published this paper.

By 2009, the first public ledger was made available for transactions by means of Bitcoin. This is the birth of the blockchain. It also led to the creation of the first lot of Bitcoins. It should be noted that they were practically worthless as the public was yet to catch on to its usefulness.

The blockchain 2.0 was developed in 2014. This enabled digital ledger technology to be implemented for transactions that went beyond financial dealings. For instance, it could be used for personal identification purposes or virtually any other type of purpose that users could consider useful.

Following the emergence of the second generation blockchain, other cryptos began to emerge. This is the case of Ethereum, Litecoin, and Ripple, among many others. In the case of Ripple, it resembles Bitcoin quite a bit though its technology makes it a lot easier to authenticate than Bitcoin. This is due to the fact that Ripple was created for the sole purpose of settling accounts, meaning facilitating transactions. It's based on a public ledger. As such, operations can be easily verified so that full transparency is ensured.

As for Ethereum, this is a separate blockchain that produces a coin called "ether." This technology allows for the creation of what are known as "smart contracts." In other words, contracts among individuals can be authenticated and enforced by means of this technology. Additionally, the Ethereum network can issue as many coins as needed without having to go through the creation process that Bitcoin has.

How Blockchain Changed Digital Money and Transactions

Considering the fact that the main purpose of the blockchain was to facilitate transactions and ensure transparency, it should be said that this type of technology has revolutionized the world. Consequently, there is a greater possibility of a decentralized financial system.

This is the underlying tenet of the blockchain and cryptocurrencies as the main purpose is to create a monetary system in which users could be free to conduct business without having to go through the supervision of a government and its monetary agencies.

Naturally, this is a revolutionary concept as governments have cracked down on activity that is outside of its jurisdiction. However, the internet is a truly vast domain in which a single institution is unable to regulate the entire number of transactions that take place.

Additionally, traditional fiat currency, even when it's used in digital format such as through e-banking, still has its limitation. For instance, it is practically impossible to issue new currency as needed, particularly when the volume of transactions picks up. This is a key factor that has limited the growth of business. And while governments can just issue as much currency as they want at a stroke of a pen, it's really not that easy. There are checks and balances that must be met in order for currency creation to take place.

Moreover, currency creation is not an act that reflects economic logic. Most of the time, monetary policy reflects political issues and considerations. As a result, monetary policy tends to be restrictive and works on a lag.

On the whole, the decentralization of currency makes it possible for individuals to conduct business freely. This implies that accounts and transactions can be settled publicly and transparently without having to limit the number of transactions.

Crypto's biggest detractors claim that cryptos lend themselves to corruption and crime. For example, terrorists can negotiate dealings by using cryptos. After all, they are anonymous as they don't require a passport for a transaction to be verified.

However, this has yet to be proven on a public ledger network. If anything, such shady transactions happen on the deep web. In this domain, there is literally no control or regulation. Nevertheless, the average citizen will never go anywhere near the dark web. So, it's safe to say that for now there is no shady business going on.

The main grievance that governments have with blockchain technology is that these transactions are not susceptible to taxation. This implies that accounts can be settled using cryptos without any proceeds going to the government in terms of taxation. This is why efforts are being made to find a means of taxing transactions made with cryptos. While there is no official ban on cryptos, most governments are reluctant to allow cryptos to be "legal," even though they are not breaking or circumventing any laws.

On the whole, the blockchain looks to become the wave of the future for business. As the world becomes more and more technologically inclined, cryptos, or digital currencies for that matter, will take over the vast majority of financial transactions. Perhaps there will still be a place for physical money. However, the outlook is that everyone on the planet will eventually have a digital wallet in which their wealth can be stored seemingly forever.

Private Vs. Public Blockchains

So far, we have talked about "the blockchain" as if there were only one in existence. However, you might be surprised to find that there are a number of blockchains in existence. Some are public such as is the case of Bitcoin, and some are private. Private blockchains are limited to a certain number of users. These users gain access through whatever means creators provide and can only transact within that blockchain using its corresponding cryptos.

This is important to note as a blockchain does not necessarily have to be open to the entire planet. The verification and authentication process can happen in a reduced group of people. The idea is that as long as everyone trusts everyone who's on the blockchain, then the blockchain serves its purpose.

The existence of private blockchains has led to the idea of countries creating their own national blockchains. These private blockchains would be limited to the citizens of a country with a national crypto in place. On the surface, this seems like a highly practical approach. However, the reality is that it would function pretty much the same as the current fiat-based currency system. And while there would be greater transparency, the fact of the matter is that the main objective of decentralization would not occur.

This is why the world strives for the implementation of truly global, public blockchains that can govern most of the transactions in the world. On the flip side, detractors claim that truly public blockchains would eliminate privacy. This is a valid consideration when you factor in that not everyone wants their purchases to be made public for the entire world to see. Perhaps it's not so much a question of trying to hide something. Still, the fact is that privacy is the biggest concern that stems from the implementation of truly public digital ledger technology.

Ultimately, there needs to be a balance. This is why having both public and private blockchains can allow users to have a greater sense of both transparency and privacy. Perhaps there needs to be levels in which transactions would be considered public while others would be considered private. These levels could be the result of consensus among citizens. However, it's important to understand that if left up to the government to regulate, the blockchain would become just as bureaucratic as the current financial system is.

In the end, digital currencies are still in their infancy. There are a number of issues that need to be worked out so that digital currencies can truly satisfy the needs of the market. Perhaps at some point down the road, this technology will be practical enough so that we can develop a truly decentralized monetary system which can provide every citizen of the world the opportunity to live on equal footing. For now, only time will tell. Yet, you have the opportunity to take advantage of the crypto space. After all, this is what this book is all about.

CHAPTER 3

Cryptocurrency Regulations

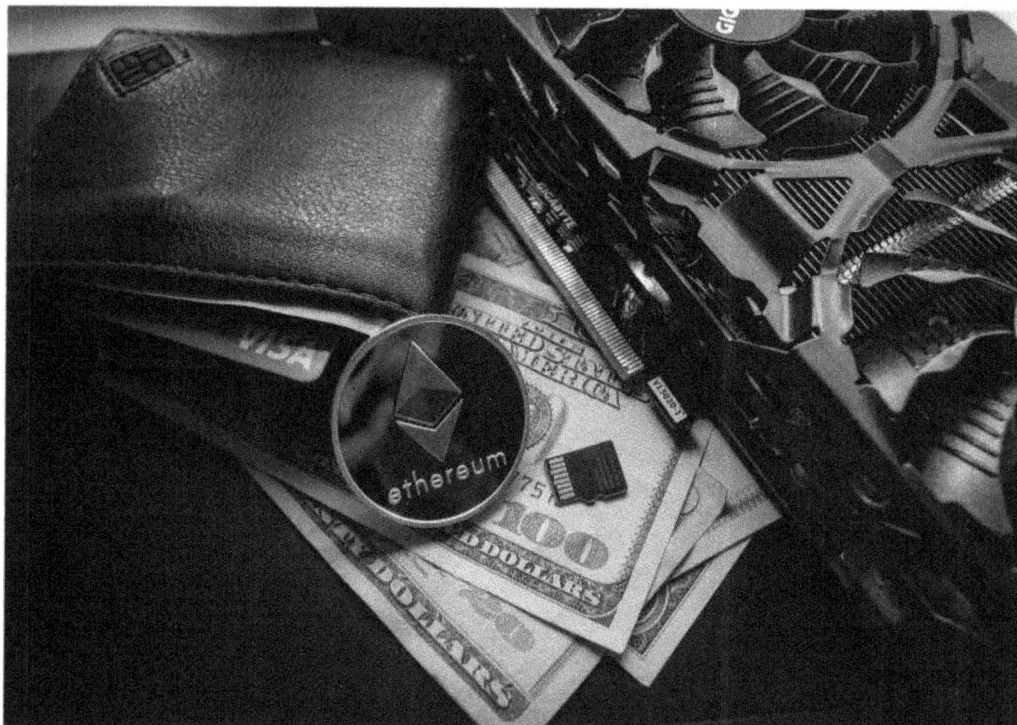

To understand the significance of cryptos, it's important to understand the nature of money and currency.

By definition, money serves as a medium of exchange. This implies that any commodity which is used as money must serve as a means of facilitating trade among all parties involved. Consequently, both buyers and sellers must agree that the commodity used to finalize a transaction is valid. For instance, if the two sides in the negotiation decided to use water as money, both sides must agree that water sufficiently represents the value that the commodity encompasses. As a result, the buyer is happy to give up their water in exchange for the goods and services negotiated. At the same time, the seller is happy to receive the water as payment for their goods and services.

Throughout history, humanity has used a number of commodities as money. However, virtually every commodity that was used had some type of issue, which made it unsustainable. Money needs to be divisible and fungible in order to actually serve as money. By "divisible," we mean that any currency which acts as money must be susceptible to division in equal parts without altering its natural composition. As for "fungible," this means that you don't necessarily need to receive the exact same unit of currency. Any other unit of currency that is of the same value will represent an equal amount of value.

To put these two points into perspective, consider the case of cattle as money. First of all, cattle are not divisible. This means that you cannot chop a cow in half to settle a payment. By the same token, not all cattle are the same. Some cattle are larger; others are fatter. This means that you cannot accept just any cattle as they do not represent the same kind of value.

Then, money is used as a store of wealth. This implies that when you hold on to it, money retains its value over time. In the case of cattle, a holder cannot keep it for a long time. In fact, cattle may simply grow old and die, thereby leaving the holder without their wealth.

Of all the commodities that humanity has used as money, the only two that have stood the test of time are gold and silver. These metals encompass all the characteristics that are needed for a commodity to function as money. That's why gold and silver have served as money for thousands of years.

However, there is a problem with physical gold and silver. In order for them to be used, they need to be mined out of the ground. This means that there is a limited supply of these metals available at any one time. Additionally, carrying a large amount of gold or silver, especially when settling a large account, can be inconvenient as it can be voluminous and heavy.

This is why countries figured out a way around it. The issuance of paper certificates to represent the value of gold and silver. Eventually, this system led to the creation of the famous "gold standard," that is, a country's currency is backed by a specific amount of gold and/or silver. In fact, this gold-backed currency system was in play until 1971. This means that up to about 40 years ago, all of the money in circulation around the world was fixed to a weight of gold.

Since then, gold and silver have been replaced by what is known as "fiat" currency. The term "fiat" refers to money issued by decree. As such, a government has the right to issue its own currency in order to for all transactions to be settled within the specific domain of that country.

This is why there is a market for foreign currency.

Since individuals do business with other individuals in other countries, there is a need to equate currencies based on their convertibility. These are the cross rates we have been referring to throughout this book.

Since fiat currency isn't backed by a physical commodity such as gold, there isn't any "real" backing behind it. Moreover, fiat currency's backing is based on the confidence that people have in it. So, as long as people believe it is valuable, it will be accepted as a means of settling accounts. When confidence falls, so does the value of the currency. This is when people stop accepting it as a means of payment and begin to demand a currency that does hold its value.

Furthermore, fiat currency is much more practical as it has led to the advancement of digital currency. As such, digital transactions can take place without the need for physical money. Although you can always go to an ATM and withdraw cash.

Still, the principles exploited in the use of digital fiat currency is what enables the creation of cryptos. Cryptos function in the same manner as regular currency insofar as it is backed by people's confidence. As long as people believe it to be an adequate store of value, they will be accepted as a means of settling accounts.

Lastly, cryptos solve one of the biggest issues that have haunted physical currency since the beginning of time. Since it does not physically exist, there is no real limit to the amount of currency that can be placed in circulation. Therefore, there could be an infinite money supply since there is no need to lug cash around. This facilitates the expansion of trade and financial services while also enabling citizens to keep their wealth store for extended periods. After all, a digital currency will never rust, break, or deteriorate over time. This makes it ideal for long-term storage.

The Decentralizing of Money

As noted earlier, the biggest advantage of cryptocurrencies is their decentralization. This means that cryptos are not subject to their issuances by a central bank or government authority. As such, cryptos are essentially created by the people and for the people.

However, this violates one of the main functions of central banks. In fact, it is a function that governments have fought very hard to impose upon their people. This is important to note as currency wasn't always issued by central banks or governments.

In fact, this is a relatively new concept.

In the past, most commercial banks could issue their own currency. In particular, banks that dominated a region could issue their own currency by way of banknotes. These banknotes could only be cashed in at the issuing bank.

The reason for these banknotes was based on the need to reduce the amount of physical gold and silver in circulation. So, bank customers could deposit their gold at a commercial bank and then issue banknotes as a means of paying other individuals. The individuals who received these notes could either cash them in for gold or use them to pay other individuals.

In a manner of speaking, it was like using a check that you received to pay someone else.

As commercial banks began issuing more and more notes, governments began cracking down on them as governments felt that commercial banks were infringing upon the sovereign right of the state to issue currency. That's why central banks came into being in the first place.

Do you see why governments aren't too crazy about cryptos?

On the whole, cryptos themselves do not infringe upon this government right. However, they are a direct competition for legal tender as folks would rather do business in a currency that is easy to use and not subject to taxation.

Herein lies the problem.

Governments aren't thrilled with the idea of cryptos gaining momentum, as this would imply accepting transactions that go beyond the traditional domain of taxing common transactions. This is why governments are yet to recognize any kind of validity of cryptocurrencies.

Furthermore, crypto breaks a central bank's monopoly over currency creation. This is what we mean by "decentralization." In fact, under the concept of the blockchain, virtually anyone can create their own currency in order to conduct any number of transactions. While this may provide unprecedented freedom, it can also cause havoc.

The reason why the proliferation of cryptos can lead to chaos is due to the lack of regulation. This means that clear rules need to be established in order for proper guidelines and procedures to be put in place. Without them, there would be no way that controversies could be solved, or rule could be enforced. Of course, the blockchain uses a set of rules which foster transparency, but the fact that there could be any number of cryptos in circulation makes it hard to keep score.

Additionally, having a large number of cryptos creates a situation in which it is hard to create a standard system of measurement. This is due to the fact that cryptos are measured differently, thereby making it hard to create a reasonable valuation for the goods and services in circulation.

Nevertheless, cryptos appear to be the largest step humankind has taken toward a fully digital monetary system that looks to decentralize government control over people's right to buy and sell the goods and services they need.

The Ban on Cryptos

The legality of cryptos is one of the hottest issues surrounding the cryptocurrency world. In essence, there are two sides to this discussion. Either you believe cryptos are legal or you don't. There really isn't any kind of middle ground in this discussion. For some folks, cryptos are perfectly legal and should not be banned. Others consider cryptos to be illegal as it is not an official government-issued currency.

However, determining the legality of cryptos boils down to a legal question that countries need to solve based on their current legal frameworks. This poses an interesting question as many countries do not outright ban cryptocurrencies. Yet, they don't explicitly authorize them either. This creates a legal vacuum that can be exploited by some unscrupulous folks.

In some countries, there is explicit legislation which either bans or authorizes the use of cryptocurrencies. In the countries in which cryptos are not explicitly outlawed, their use is limited to a certain set of transactions and situations. In other cases, their ban is total. This implies that anyone who is caught using cryptos for business purposes can be subject to prosecution.

While that may sound harsh, it makes perfect sense when you consider that governments will do everything they can to enforce their sovereignty over a country's monetary systems.

So, let's take a look at specific cases in which cryptocurrencies are considered legal.

In the European Union (EU), Bitcoin is considered to be a legal means of payment. However, it is not considered to be a currency. As such, it can be used to settle accounts and make payments despite the fact that it is not considered to be eligible for VAT when converting regular fiat currency to Bitcoin. However, transactions settle in Bitcoin are eligible for payment of VAT or sales taxes.

As for the G7 countries, guidance was issued in 2013 for companies dealing with digital currencies. While the G7 resolution did not explicitly grant permission for the use of digital-based currencies, companies were asked to follow applicable legislation in order to ensure proper adherence to financial regulations.

Interestingly enough, the United States declared Bitcoin to be legal in 2013 though it does not receive the status of a currency. Rather, it is considered to be a commodity and trades alongside other similar commodities like gold and silver. This implies that you can buy and sell Bitcoin through financial instruments as you would any other type of commodity.

In Canada, Bitcoin is legal and regulated by applicable legislation. However, there is a banking ban on the use of Bitcoin, meaning that customers are not permitted to conduct transactions using credit cards for the purchase of cryptos.

One clear case is that of Costa Rica. Costa Rica's laws do not recognize Bitcoin as a currency, as it is not backed by the government. By the same token, it is not illegal as it does not infringe any laws. Therefore, it's up to individual merchants to decide if they accept Bitcoin, or not.

In contrast, Bolivia and Ecuador have issued strict legislation banning Bitcoin outright. Other countries that have outlawed Bitcoin include Pakistan, Morocco, Egypt, and Algeria.

Ultimately, accepting Bitcoin (or any other crypto for that matter) as a means of payment appears to be a decision left up to individual merchants. This bodes well for the future of cryptos unless there is specific legislation down the road that reverses the current acceptance of cryptos.

State-Backed Cryptocurrencies

The idea of a state-backed cryptocurrency seems far-fetched at this point. In fact, most governments would rather not go near cryptos as they would much rather continue the issuance of fiat currency. However, the debate regarding governments getting into the crypto market has gained traction in the last few years.

One perspective on this matter is based on the premise of having governments issue their own cryptos so that private citizens are unable to do so. As such, the idea of government-issued cryptos seems to make a great deal of sense when you consider the practical use that could be given to such currencies.

In particular, the idea behind a state-backed crypto lies in moving away from physical currency into an entirely digital monetary system. When you think about it, we're a lot closer to that reality than you think. In fact, a great deal of financial transactions are just numbers of a computer screen. While you can still go down to the bank and get cash, the likelihood of that happening becomes less and less over time.

The fact is that it's much more practical to pay bills and make transactions by hitting a few keystrokes rather than carrying a wallet full of cash. Moreover, technologically-oriented folks would much rather use their phones and computers to do business rather than having to go through the complications of handling physical cash.

Still, the prospect of governments actually getting into the crypto market is still a long way away. One country that has expressed interest in an official crypto is China oddly enough. Given the fact that China is very much on the cutting edge of technology, it makes sense that they would be interested in issuing its own cryptocurrency. In fact, there has been talk of a gold-backed cryptocurrency. This crypto would be nothing more than digits on a computer screen. Nevertheless, the backing of this currency would be a fixed amount of gold. The purpose of this is to create confidence in the crypto itself, that is, give investors the impression that they are not being swindled by computer code.

Ultimately, it remains to be seen if this type of cryptocurrency would make sense. But there is no doubt that a cryptodollar or cryptoeuro is on the horizon. It's only a matter of time before governments wake up and realize there isn't much they can do to stop the emergence of cryptos. So, it's best to get with the program and take control before it's too late for governments.

The Future of Digital Currency

There is no question that digital currency is the way of the future. The question that is on the table is what digital currency will be like. The likeliest scenario at this point would be some kind of migration from traditional physical fiat currencies into a purely digital format.

As it stands, this would not be practical in much of the world. The majority of countries in the world still rely heavily on cash for the bulk of their transactions. And while the use of digital financial tools is rising, there is still a long way to go.

More and more, individual citizens are using digital means such as credit cards, e-banking, and third-party services like PayPal, Apple Pay, or Venmo, among many others. In fact, if you really tried to live a cashless life, you could certainly do it. Of course, some of your options would be limited. Still, there are plenty of ways in which you could go cashless.

When you think about it, the future of digital currency is wide open. In this case, though, we're not entirely clear what that future will look like. The emergence of the FinTech industry has provided investors with a clearer idea of what they can expect down the road. Still, there is a long way to go. The transition from physical currency to completely digital transactions requires the construction of a robust infrastructure that can handle the vast number of transactions that occur every day.

This means that a fully digital world would truly be something out of a science fiction movie. At the moment, it might seem unfathomable to think that not a single penny would exist, but then again, is that so hard to imagine?

It's important to keep in mind that the time to get into this market is now. Just like those savvy individuals who recognized an opportunity in Bitcoin way back in 2009, you have the opportunity to get in on the early days of this growing industry. You have the opportunity to really make your mark on the world by engaging the future of digital currency.

It's only a matter of time before governments realize that the blockchain, among other types of digital ledger technology, is the best way to ensure transparency among all people. It's a way of keeping folks accountable while establishing clear rules. So, it's best to get in on the action now, before it's too late. Once all the cards have been dealt with, it will be very hard for investors to make substantial gains. If experience has taught us anything, it's that having the vision to recognize emerging technologies before they become mainstream is the most effective way of capitalizing on a new trend. This is why we would encourage you to embrace cryptos before they take over the world market... for good!

CHAPTER 4

Trading Cryptocurrencies

In this chapter, we are going to take a look at more specific aspects of cryptos and how you can get started with the fundamentals of trading cryptos. Additionally, we are going to discuss some very interesting issues which don't normally get addressed in regular investment literature.

In this regard, investing in cryptos can be a bit of a challenge. There are a number of factors that play into the valuation of cryptos while also making it tough to consider the importance of investor psyche. Consequently, you need to consider the importance that psychological factors have on the overall valuation of cryptos and how they can influence price and investment decisions.

In order to understand the valuation of cryptos, it's important to understand the dynamics of market forces and how they influence the price of any commodity and not just cryptos. As a result, we need to focus on a series of issues that underscore the importance of fundamentals in market conditions.

Also, we are going to specifically focus on Bitcoin, as this is the most commonly traded crypto. It's also the crypto that has gained the most notoriety around the world. Even though it has a rather limited supply, it's present all over the world. Consequently, investors from all walks of life are interested in seeing how they can make money off this little-understood commodity.

Why Is Bitcoin So Expensive?

This is a question for the ages.

In order to answer this question, it's important to look at Bitcoin as a commodity and not as a currency. This is a fundamental distinction as currencies and commodities trade quite differently.

In the case of currencies, these are subject to exchange rates. This means that you essentially convert one currency into another at a determined ratio. When you travel, you exchange your country's currency for that of the local currency of the country you are visiting. For most travelers, they first need to convert their country's currency into a major one such as US Dollars or Euros and then into the local currency of the county they are visiting.

When you speculate in currency exchange, you can make money from the increase or decrease in value of one currency in comparison to another. This is what the FOREX market is all about. Hence, the FOREX market has a completely different dynamic as the traditional stock market does.

With that in mind, looking at Bitcoin as a commodity means that it trades in the same way precious metals, agricultural goods, oil, and other goods that fall under this category. In addition, Bitcoin is also subject to the various investment vehicles that are available for commodities such as Exchange Traded Funds (ETFs), futures contracts, options, and straight buying and selling in the spot market.

Based on this premise, Bitcoin's valuation is rather straightforward. Simply put, there are investors who are willing to pay more than others for the right to hold Bitcoin. Moreover, the valuation of Bitcoin resembles that typical "bubble" that you often hear about on financial news channels.

In essence, a bubble consists of investors who want to get into an investment but without really understanding the underlying value of that investment. All they understand is that this investment is a great way to make money. As a result, they want to get in any way they can. That drives up the prices as holders of the asset are prepared to sell to the highest bidder.

This is exactly what happened to Bitcoin.

As investor realized the incredible potential of cryptocurrencies, they figured that getting into cryptos any way they could, would enable them to clean up when they eventually sold. This was true for the investors who got in early.

Way back in 2009, you couldn't give Bitcoin away. When it first began trading, it went for roughly $2 a coin. Yes, that's right, *two dollars*. It would take years for Bitcoin to get off the ground. When the blockchain and the potential for cryptocurrencies to become known, investors were willing to take a gamble on it. Those who had originally purchased at around $2 a coin, made a massive killing when coins began to sell at $200 apiece. From there, more and more investors had to get in.

Now, the reason why Bitcoin's price soared was its relative scarcity. Because of this, investors were willing to practically pay anything for a coin. But like all markets, it eventually leveled off. The ceiling for Bitcoin hit $20,000 a coin. At this point, the price simply become prohibitive for most investors.

Then, demand began to dry up.

Naturally, those who had already made a killing were reluctant to get back in. After all, why would they invest more money if they had already cashed out? This is where Bitcoin's price began to fall. From $20,000 a coin, it fell back down to about $2,000 a coin. At this price point, investors sought to get back in. Then, Bitcoin made a come up and jumped back up to $10,000 before falling back down.

Since the great boom and bust of Bitcoin, it generally trades between $5,000 to $8,000 a coin. On the whole, this fluctuation is due to the fact that investors seek safer assets when things get tough in the stock market. Alongside traditional safe-haven assets such as gold and bonds, investors are now looking at Bitcoin as a safe haven. Consequently, its price will go up and down based on investor demand.

How Is Trading Cryptocurrency Different From Regular Forex Trading?

Again, we must go back to the fact that Bitcoin trades like a commodity. As such, Bitcoin does not behave like a currency in the manner the Swiss Franc does. Bitcoin behaves in the same way that gold, coffee, and natural gas do. As long as there are investors who seek to purchase it, there will be a demand.

Let's take a look at an example of how a commodity is traded on the open market.

Oil is traded on the international market at a spot price. This means that the unit in which oil is traded (a barrel) has a specific price today. That price is used to negotiate the value of the contract. For instance, let's assume that a barrel of oil costs $50. This is today's price, and hence it is the spot price. When an investor wishes to purchase oil, they multiply the price by the number of barrels. That becomes the value of the contract.

However, oil cannot be delivered immediately; that is, it cannot be bought and then handed over right away. In the specific case of oil, a purchase made today is delivered roughly three months into the future. The same goes for agricultural products, metals, and practically any other commodity which doesn't already exist.

So, you are essentially purchasing a contract that's good for the delivery of the oil you have bought. This physical delivery will take place at the date specified in the terms of the contact. Please note that there are experts in the oil trade who have never even seen a barrel of oil in front of them. Yet, they trade in oil, make considerable amounts of money, and generate sound profits simply by trading contracts.

Additionally, the futures market is where commodities are bought and sold with a future date in mind. This means that you are locking in today's price (or whatever price you negotiate) on a deal that will take place at any point in the future. For instance, instead of the traditional 3-month time period, oil producers may negotiate contracts 6 months or even one year into the future. The reason for this is that these producers need cash to keep the lights on today. Investors trust these companies, and so they are willing to give them an advance on the overall value of the contract.

This is a general overview of how commodities are traded. This is an overview of how you can expect to trade Bitcoin on the open market. There is a spot market for Bitcoin, and then there is a futures market. When you put them together, there is a healthy "paper market" for them. We use the term "paper" as you are not dealing with the real thing; you are just selling the rights to it.

There is one other financial instrument that is used for trading commodities, which you need to be aware of: exchange traded funds (ETFs).

An ETF is basically an agreement under which a group of investors all pool their money and buy into a given commodity or group of commodities. These funds are managed by a firm, individual, or large financial institution to invest in a given product. The proceeds are then divided among the investor, while the investment firm keeps a percentage as a commission for their troubles. Some ETFs can be purchased through your regular broker, while others are "rich" clubs in which you need a certain net worth to get in.

Crypto ETFs have become popular in recent years. These investments give the general public exposure to cryptos without having to shell out $10,000 for a single coin. As such, small investors can get into the action even if they only invest a fraction of the cost for a single Bitcoin. Naturally, their share of the action is less. Still, it provides exposure to this market even when you may be just starting out with a few hundred dollars.

As a result, the main difference between crypto markets and FOREX is that cryptos are traded like commodities while FOREX trades like currency. With FOREX, you are swapping one currency for another at a determined exchange rate. This does not happen with cryptos. In addition, FOREX is a highly volatile market meaning that shifts in exchange rates can happen quite suddenly. And while regular commodities are subject to sharp movements in the market, the difference can be significant in the FOREX market is a very short timeframe.

So, you might be asking yourself, "are cryptos better than FOREX?"

The answer to that depends on what you are looking to gain. Frankly, FOREX requires much more active participation on the part of the investor. On the other hand, cryptos don't require a great deal of participation, especially if you take a passive approach, such as investing through an ETF. At the end of the day, it boils down on how much involvement you want in a specific investment. Hence, cryptos could be your best choice especially if you are simply looking to make money on the side.

The Best Cryptocurrencies to Trade

When looking to invest in cryptos, it's natural to be overwhelmed by the large number of coins out there. You might be enticed to take a flyer on coins value at a few dollars apiece. Who knows, they might turn out to be the next Bitcoin. But the likelihood of that happening is rather slim. Still, you could find some hidden gems if you look close enough.

But if you seek real value, then the following list will help you get ahead of the game.

1. **Bitcoin**. By far, this is the most popular crypto and the one with the most developed market. You can find all sorts of instruments ranging from the straight-up spot market to futures and ETFs. If you wish to gain exposure to it, but don't have the capital needed to make a significant investment, then an ETF might be the way to go.

2. **Ripple**. This is an affordable crypto that seems to be on the rise. In 2019, payment giant MoneyGram began using Ripple's blockchain to conduct transfers. This bodes well for Ripple as the coin itself may not be the most attractive aspect, but its proprietary technology is.

3. **Litecoin**. This crypto is generally mentioned in the same category as Bitcoin. While it doesn't have nearly as much exposure, you can certainly get in on the action. Individual Litecoins trade for less than a hundred dollars and are generally considered to have a great upside. It's already made a name for itself in the market. So, you can have reasonable assurance that you won't go wrong with this investment.

4. **Ethereum.** This is another of the big-league cryptos. The reason why Ethereum has such an incredible upside is due to the fact that its blockchain can be used for a multitude of projects. This makes its potential unlimited. While trading at less than $200 apiece, Ethereum is still affordable enough for newbies to get into the crypto space without breaking the bank.

5. **Neo.** Perhaps you haven't heard too much about Neo. It's relatively new on the scene, but it does hold some upside to it as it is an open-source technology. As such, it is a community-driven coin that seeks to optimize the flow of the digital economy. Be on the lookout for this one. Early investors saw their value double from around $7.50 a coin. Since then, it's settled to around $11.00 a coin. That's a pretty solid gain in the crypto world.

6. **Zcash**. Zcash's biggest advantage is its privacy protocols. It offers a higher degree of privacy than Bitcoin while enabling users to avoid tracking by government or private companies. It does have a fixed supply at the moment, 21 million coins, meaning that it does have the potential to spike in value. As of 2019, Zcash peaked at $112 per coin. Nevertheless, keep an eye out for this coin as it could follow the path of Bitcoin.

7. **Stellar**. This is a relative newcomer to the scene. It's been around since 2014 and aims to replace the aging SWIFT international banking network. It looks to create tokens that could facilitate international banking transactions in such a way that times could be reduced significantly.

8. **Cardano**. You may not have heard of this one. That's because it's only been around since 2015. However, it promises to deliver functionality for large-scale financial operations. Overall, it could lead to the possibility of a layered technology that would make updating seamless.

9. **Tron**. Tron is another newcomer. It's been around since 2017 and looks to provide a global network that would facilitate entertainment. This would enable free interaction among users. It has the potential to take over current world leaders like Netflix. Content creators would have a platform in which they could share and monetize their content freely and easily.

10. **Ontology**. This platform looks to integrate multiple chains. As such, it seeks to create simple solutions so that businesses can create ways of improving the reach of their business. So far, the Ontology network has a maximum output of 1 billion tokens.

Trends of Cryptocurrencies

To say that cryptos are on the rise is an understatement. Cryptos are clearly here to stay. The question then becomes: how to take advantage of cryptos?

To take advantage of the growing trend in cryptos, you need to play a dual role, both as a user and an investor. Firstly, if you already make use of digital banking services, then you are already well on your way to becoming a crypto user. The only difference between your current online banking and cryptos is the currency system itself.

This means that we can't really determine what using Bitcoin, Ethereum, or Litecoin will be like in terms of prices. It could be that buying a new car will cost you 10 Litecoins as opposed to $10,000. Nevertheless, these are minor changes when considering the functionality of cryptos.

It should be noted that the prices of cryptos do tend to fluctuate quite a bit. This is mainly due to the fact that these trade as commodities do. Thus, it's not easy to maintain stability in their pricing. Moreover, demand for cryptos at the moment is limited to a handful of investors. Even when the average user wishes to enter the crypto space, they may not necessarily have the means to do so. As a result, it can be somewhat complicated to get into the market at this point.

It is clear though, that the outlook for cryptos is a bright one. While we can't be sure about the amount of time it will take for cryptos to really catch on, the fact of the matter is that they are here to stay. So, it is now a matter of capitalizing on the upswing.

Getting Into Cryptocurrencies

If you are ready to take the plunge into crypto investing, then you should know that it isn't quite like picking up the phone and calling a broker. While you might find that some financial investment institutions do offer some kind of crypto investment fund, your best bet is to stay away from them.

To get into cryptos, there are two main ways. One is to purchase them directly from another user. This is like buying any kind of asset. All you do is pay the agreed price, and that's the end of it. However, these transactions are often fraudulent. So, you need to find a means of ensuring that the people you are dealing with are reputable. Otherwise, you may fall for a scam.

This is why the second way, and the best way, is to go through a coin exchange. These are online platforms in which you can buy and sell your coins easily and with the assurance that you are dealing with verified users. These exchanges include Coinbase, GDAx, and Bitfinex. These exchanges promote the fair exchange of coins while allowing users to make payments using credit cards and payment services like Apple Pay or PayPal. Of course, there are processing fees and commissions attached to these exchanges, so do keep them in mind.

The good thing about these exchanges is that they allow you to buy fractions of a coin. As such, you can buy a piece of a Bitcoin. This allows you to get into the action without having to shell out $10,000 for a single coin. If the price goes up, you make money. If the price goes down, then sit tight and wait for the rebound.

On the whole, getting into cryptos is quite easy. Plus, you don't have to deal with the number of regulations that come with regular investments in stocks and other financial instruments. Unless you have to know that you are dealing with a reputable individual, it's always best to go through and exchange. You have the assurance that you won't be swindled by an unscrupulous individual.

CHAPTER 5

Analysis Of Crypto Trades

When looking to get started trading cryptos, it's important to become acquainted with the indicators that will help you track the progress and development of the price action related to cryptocurrencies. On the whole, these indicators are meant to be part of your technical analysis toolkit. They will provide you with the analytics you need to make rational decisions based on solid data. These data can help you complement your hunches. After all, it's important to have your instincts confirmed by the data. Otherwise, you may find yourself following a gut feeling that may, or may not, have any reasoning behind it.

If you are familiar with technical analysis in either stocks or FOREX, then you will find these analytics tools to be quite familiar. They are essentially the same though they are translated and honed for their use in the crypto market. Still, the fundamentals are quite similar. So, you should have no trouble adapting them accordingly.

In case you are brand new to the crypto market, fear not. The explanations provided in this chapter will enable you to get the most out of the information you will find in the charts and graphs described herein. Best of all, you will become quickly adept at identifying trends and patterns in the information seen in the charts and graphs in question. So, it's just a question of taking the time to review the fundamentals in order to get the most out of the information found in the technical analysis data pertaining to the crypto market.

Setting Up Indicators

The most important indicator that you need to become familiar with is **price**. That's the main indicator that will tell you how a particular crypto is doing. There is no question that price is your biggest friend. If you are able to make the right analysis of price action, you should be able to make sound decisions based on the amount of data available to you.

Let's consider this situation:

Price fluctuations are the result of the interaction between supply and demand. If you get into a crypto that is in high demand, the chances of you making good money are higher than if you get into a crypto that doesn't have a high demand. In such a case, you would need to be more patient. In contrast, cryptos that have a higher demand can be traded a lot more easily.

On the other hand, you might have a crypto that has a limited supply. In such cases, even when there isn't such high demand, the fact that there is a limited supply makes it more valuable. Such cryptos can offer you a good opportunity to make some money even when you may not be keen on holding onto your position for a long time.

When looking at price, please ensure that you have a look at the various timeframes that are available to you. Often, looking at a specific timeframe will only offer you a snapshot of what's actually going on in the market. In this case, you might be faced with a situation in which you are basing your assessments on incomplete data. So, it's always good to go back and review the data you have analyzed at various timeframes. This will enable you to get a better idea of the crypto's overall behavior patterns.

Another important indicator is known as the "moving average." This measure is calculated by tracking the average price of a crypto over a certain time period. This indicator can be calculated at any timeframe though the most common measurement is hourly. In the case of highly traded markets such as FOREX, it can be calculated on a minute-by-minute basis. However, this is not commonly done in crypto as cryptos don't have nearly as high trading volume. As a result, an hourly chart provides you with accurate information on the crypto's performance.

The moving average tracks the average between buy and sell prices. This is represented by candlesticks. These are the bars and move up and down the chart. Each candlestick represents the opening price at the bottom, the closing price at the top, and the length of the candlestick's body represents the margin between both prices. The longer the candlestick, the greater the difference.

Typically, the most common measure used for the purpose of tracking trend is the 10-day moving average. This average will tell you the average price of a crypto over a period of 10 days. This timeframe can then be further broken down into hourly segments. These hourly segments can help you pick up on any patterns that might be visible at certain times of day. It may seem incredible, but the time of day you trade has a significant impact on the results you stand to gain.

Other longer timeframes include the 20-day, 50-day, and 100-day moving average. All of these longer timeframes can be used to determine if there are any cyclical patterns in the price action of a crypto. For instance, there might be seasonal influence such as a downturn during summer vacation.

When looking into the technical analysis of cryptos, trading volume is an important indicator. By "trading volume," we are referring to the number of transactions that are completed during a specific time period. This indicator provides you with an idea of how commonly traded a crypto can be. In addition, trading volume is a good indicator that can determine the rise in demand for a specific crypto. When trading volume picks up, it can serve as a signal that more investors are becoming interested in any given crypto. As a result, you can make more trades, and thereby greater profits, based on the increased amount of movement in the crypto itself.

How to Analyze the Market

Analyzing the crypto market is done through the use of technical analysis tools. Unless you have access to a number of traders and investors, you won't be able to get a good feel for the market unless you look at the data.

Now, if you had access to investors and traders, you could simply talk to them and gauge the market. Even then, you would still be going on purely subjective data as one investor's sentiment may differ greatly from another. So, it's a question of ensuring that you have the numbers in plain view.

When it comes to analyzing the market, it's a question of understanding trends, ranges, and significant levels. These three items, in unison, will help you get a good idea of where the market is at the moment and where it may be headed down the road. As a result, you can't simply take one indicator; you need to look into all three indicators to help you get a good understanding of where the market will ultimately land.

In this regard, it's important to have access to as much technical data as you can. So, the first challenge becomes where to find the right data you need to conduct market analysis. There are many sources out there. So, it's best to have a discriminating eye when it comes to the information you are basing your decisions on.

Some of the major business news outlets such as Bloomberg, CNN, Money Watch, among others, may report on cryptos only as far as major news related to main cryptos such as Bitcoin and Ethereum. If anything, you may find information on crypto pricing specifically related to Bitcoin. Beyond that, getting detailed information can be a bit tough. This is why you need to consult website and market sources which are devoted especially to the crypto space.

Two sites that offer good information on the crypto space are CoinDesk and Coinbase. Both of these sites offer comprehensive information on pricing, volume, and supply. They can be a great place to start as far as getting updated information regarding the most relevant coins. Since there are thousands of coins in the market at the moment, it's virtually impossible to report on all of them. As such, you can get information on the most traded coins in addition to some lesser-known ones.

In the case of CoinDesk, this is an information service. As a result, you can expect to find a great deal of information regarding all things crypto. In this site, you can find just about everything you need to know with regard to the market. This is a great place to find current information. Also, it is a go-to reference site for crypto investors.

As for Coinbase, we mentioned earlier that this is an exchange. Therefore, you can buy and sell coins here. Consequently, Coinbase offers a great deal of information pertaining to the cryptos traded on their exchange. In this regard, the information may not be the broadest as it is essentially limited to the coins they offer. Nevertheless, there is a good deal of information. So, you can't go wrong with Coinbase.

Based on this, you can analyze the market in such a way that you can recognize the main indicators pertaining to the overall patterns of crypto prices. So, let's take a look at three indicators that you can deduce from the charts and graphs available to you on crypto pricing.

Trend in Price Action

In essence, trend is the direction in which the price is heading. Thus, using technical data on price action will allow you to determine this direction. On the whole, you can spot a trend just by looking at a chart. Price charts usually reflect price using a line graph. No other types of graphs are used as it is very difficult to graphically represent price using any other means.

When you look at a price chart, you'll see quite a bit of points. Some go up, and some go down. Generally speaking, this does not represent trend itself as the price action may indicate a great deal of fluctuation. Nevertheless, you can determine trend by taking a closer look at the information contained in the chart.

You can do this by looking at the direction in which the curve is moving. In some cases, the curve appears to be moving upward. This is known as a "bullish" trend. Then, you may spot the curve moving in a downward direction. This is known as a "bearish" trend.

A bullish trend means that the price is moving upward. As a result, the crypto in question is gaining in value in relation to Dollars, or perhaps another currency. On the other hand, a bearish trend means that the crypto is losing value in relation to another currency or crypto.

Determining the actual trend of the data can be done in two ways. The first is the trendline that is generated by the chart itself. Most price charts do this automatically. Otherwise, you would have to take the data in table form, input it into a spreadsheet program like Microsoft Excel, and then calculate your own trendline. While doing these calculations yourself is more time-consuming, you can be certain about the numbers you see when you do the math yourself.

Another way in which you can determine the trend in a data set is by joining the lowest point of a curve with its highest point with a straight line. The line will reveal an upward or downward slope. This is the trend. Then, you can see the various points in which the line intersects with the markings on the chart. These are all potential price points that you can use to determine your buy or sell points. It's important to note that this approach is not 100% accurate as you are simply making a manual trace. However, it is very useful when determining trend in a data set. Plus, it's great when you are simply looking at data and don't have a lot of time to actually sit down to crunch the numbers.

Of course, it's best to have an automatically generated trendline by the chart itself. Nevertheless, the methods that we have outlined here will help you to spot trend easily and effectively.

Ranges or Bands in Price

When you hear the term "range" or "band," you need to think about price action within a specific upper and lower limit. This means that prices do not exceed these limits. For instance, XYT crypto is trading "in a band." This means that the lower limit of the band is $1 while the upper limit is $5. This implies that you can expect to see its price range anywhere from $1 to $5. However, you cannot expect to see the price fall below $1 or exceed $5. If that were to happen, then you could be experiencing an unusual opportunity.

There are times when a crypto trades in a "narrow band." This means that the price does not move very much either way. For example, the price can range from $1 to $1.05. The range here is 5 cents on the Dollar. Depending on the usual price action, the band could be even narrower. Sometimes, the band is so narrow that changes are measured in amounts less than a penny.

Now, you might be thinking, "how can you make money if a crypto is making less than a penny?"

The answer to that is numbers.

You see, when you trade in large amounts, say hundreds or even thousands of coins, then you can make some significant gains. Let's assume that the gain on a coin has been a penny. Yet, you sell 10,000 of them. That's a $100 profit. That may not seem overwhelming, but it is certainly profitable when you are able to make the same trade over and over again. When you multiply $100 over say, 10 or 12 transactions, now you have about a $1,000 in your pocket.

To identify that a crypto is trading in a band, you can look for one of two types of trendlines.

The first is a horizontal trendline that is moving sideways. This means that it has very little to no upward or downward slope. If it is completely flat, then you have a crypto that might be moving in an extremely narrow margin. To take advantage of this trend, you would need to go back in time to see where the price of this crypto was sitting. It could be that it dropped, it is now trading sideways and perhaps gaining momentum before taking off. On the other hand, it could be that it climbed, leveled off and may drop back down. The important thing to notice is the direction it was headed prior to leveling off. This can give you some indication of what's to come.

The second type of trendline is a curve that fluctuates up and down in the same range. This means that there is some predictability in the levels the curve will hit. When this occurs, you can be relatively sure of how far up the price will rise, and then how far down the price will fall. Under this type of model, you can safely plot your entry and exit points. You can take advantage of this band by entering at the lowest point and selling at the highest. You may not be profiting a great deal on individual trades, but you might be able to really make some good money by exploiting that band multiple times over.

Significant Levels: Resistance and Support

One of the most important aspects of recognizing trading patterns is understanding significant levels. When we discuss these levels, we are focusing specifically on support and resistance levels. These are vitally important when considering the importance they bear on the overall way of determining price action.

Let's start by discussing what a "support level" is. In essence, a support level is the bottom or "floor" in the price of a crypto. This means that the price action will drop to this price level but not go any lower. This is important to note as support levels generally serve as a psychological barrier in which investors feel comfortable entering the market. This level serves as the base from which price action then reverses trend (usually downward) and then begins to climb back up to the high point.

It should be noted that support levels are not ironclad. This means that it is quite possible that the price will break through the floor. When this occurs, a new support level may be set. As such, you need to be keen on the price action. If you are holding on to a crypto during a breakthrough, you may end up having to hold on to the coins longer than anticipated as you wait for the price to recoup.

The high point of a price action data set is known as a "resistance level." By "resistance," we mean that investors are reluctant to pay more than a certain price for a crypto. At this point, most investors being to liquidate their position. As such, the trend reverses and begins a downward slope all the way back down to the support level. Like support, resistance is a psychological barrier in which investors feel satisfied selling their coins. However, if demand is high, investors may decide to hold on longer in hopes of getting a higher price.

When price surpasses a resistance level, you have what is known as a "breakout." A breakout is an investor's dream come true. When the price of a coin breaks out, there is no telling how high it can go. As such, you may find that if price surpasses your expectations by a wide margin. However, it should be noted that breakouts are rather uncommon. So, it's important to spot the signs so that you can ride that wave.

On the whole, this interaction between support and resistance levels can be clearly observed when a coin is trading in a band. The price rises to its resistance level and bounces back down all the way to the floor and then rebounds back up to its ceiling (resistance level). This can happen multiple times over the course of a trading day or even multiple days. This level of predictability can make it very easy to make consistent profits. So, it's definitely worth keeping in mind.

CHAPTER 6

Developing Trading Algorithms

When you read about developing trading algorithms, you will generally run into a very technical discussion on coding and software programming. Yes, trading algorithms do involve coding. This means that if you wanted to fully automate your trading, you would have to have the requisite IT skills needed to program the computer to do what you want it to do.

In fact, large institutional investors invest the money needed to produce these algorithms. The reason for this is that these large investment firms would rather pay a programmer once to develop a program rather than pay a broker over and over to trade for them.

Additionally, trading algorithms allow investors to automate their strategies. This means that there is no need for a human to be constantly entering information. The machine takes care of the process. However, there is still a need for human oversight, especially if things aren't going well.

As for retailer investors, that is, investors who have smaller investment capital, using algorithmic trading doesn't mean you need a degree in computer science or pay a ton of cash to a software developer. You can develop your own algorithms based on your knowledge and experience. As a result, you can make the most of your talents and abilities along with reliable data. This is why we are going to explore how you can make your trading algorithm so that you can facilitate trading. It should be noted that the principles described here apply, not just to cryptos, but to all financial assets. This means that these concepts can be extrapolated to stocks, FOREX, and commodities, among others.

Developing or Fine-Tuning a Strategy

The first thing you need in order to get started with algorithmic trading is to develop a strategy. This means that you need to know what you want to do even before you begin devising the nuts and bolts of your algorithm.

There are two main approaches that you can follow when it comes to devising your own trading algorithm.

The first is known as "high-frequency trading" or HFT. In HFT, what you are essentially doing is making the same trade over and over. What this allows you to do is make a profit on multiple transactions within a short timeframe. This leads you to multiply profits in quick succession so that they add up over time.

On the whole, HFT implies that you make small returns on each transaction. However, the high number of transactions conducted adds up, leading you to accumulate a significant return. This type of trading is very good for assets that are trading in a band. As such, if you find that your coin of choice is trading in a rather predictable band, you can exploit this trading to make sense for you. In the end, you rack up small profits, but multiply them over the total number of transactions conducted.

The other approach you can apply in this case is value investing. Value investing consists of finding undervalued coins which have the potential to rebound. In this case, you observe a coin that is trading below its usual market value. Then, you sell when the time is right.

This type of trading approach requires a good deal of research as you need to understand both the usual value of a coin in addition to its dynamic. For example, you have a coin that generally trades for $1. However, you find that its valuation suddenly falls to about $0.95. Upon seeing this, you realize that you are getting a good deal at this point. So, you decide to scoop it up in hopes that its valuation will return to its average of $1. Since the coin is undervalued (there are many reasons why this can happen), all you need to do is sell at $1 or slightly above it to make a profit.

This approach requires careful planning and attention to detail, even though the transaction itself is rather straightforward. The main thing here is to keep a close eye on the value of the various coins you are tracking. Once you find an undervalued coin, you pounce on it. When the price goes back up, you can sell for a profit.

It is really that simple. The hard part is finding the right coins at the right price. Therefore, this approach does not allow you to make a large number of transactions. In fact, the number of transactions you would be making is far less than in HFT.

Also, value investing is more of a manual process. However, you can use algorithmic trading to help you spot the values that you want in order to help you automate the process. As such, you won't have to pour over charts all day long to find what you seek. All you need to do is set up the right price points.

Now, the good news about algorithmic trading is that trading platforms allow you to enter the parameters of the deal you want to make happen. This is great because you can simply enter the entry and exit points, and you are good to go.

In the specific case of FOREX, trading platforms are well-equipped to serve this type of purpose. You can fully automate your trading system by entering the parameters that you want. If the price action hits these parameters, the deal is executed. If not, the deal does not happen. This can certainly help you stay on top of a situation, especially when you are not planning to be physically at your computer.

The caveat to algorithmic trading is that you cannot simply set it up and forget about it. You need to check in on it every once in a while. Usually, this might mean every hour or so. When you fail to check your automatic trading setups, the algorithm can run amok. This is especially true when trading volume picks up. If this is the case, then you might end up triggering the opposite effect of what you wish to achieve.

For instance, you have set up a very low entry point as you expect to pounce on a valuable coin. And while the entry point is triggered, the exit point is not. This means that your sell price is never hit. Thus, the sale of the coin never happens. Thus, you end up holding on to the coin much longer than anticipated. To make matters worse, the price keeps dropping. Since you weren't paying attention, the value keeps dropping and dropping, thus costing you a larger amount of money.

Do you see why you need to keep tabs on your automated positions?

Of course, this might be a bit of an extreme scenario. Nevertheless, it does happen. So, it's best to always keep tabs on any open positions you may have.

Making Use of Trendlines

As we have discussed throughout this book, trend is an integral part of your trading strategy. So, it only makes sense to automate this part of the process. Earlier, we talked about how you can manually calculate trendlines to ensure that the data you are analyzing is right. While this is certainly valid, the fact of the matter is that most investors don't have the time to sit down and pour over charts and tables. Sure, there is a great sense of satisfaction that comes with running the numbers yourself. But when it comes to trading cryptos, time really is money.

The easiest way to calculate trendlines is to simply enable this function in the charts you generate. This is, by far, the easier way. Best of all, this is done automatically for you. So, you don't have to actually worry about generating trendlines.

Once you have generated trendlines, you can use them to determine entry and exit points as part of your strategy. For instance, you can set up an entry point at the exact point where a bearish trendline touches the support level. By the same token, you can set up an exit point right when a bullish trendline touches on a resistance level.

You can easily spot these in the charts you generate. Then, all you need to do is enter these points in your trade configuration. This will alert the platform to execute these deals when these points are triggered.

That's all.

Of course, keep tabs to make sure the price action is trending in the direction you have identified. If something should go wrong, don't hesitate to pull the plug. Please bear in mind that it's always best to cut your losses as soon as possible.

Acceleration of Trend

One important aspect about trend is the pace on which it is moving. By "pace," we're referring to the time it will take for a given price point to be hit. A good rule of thumb to keep in mind here is that the sharper the slope, the faster the time. This means that a trendline that is essentially horizontal will take far longer to hit certain points compared to one that's practically vertical. Of course, perfectly horizontal and vertical trendlines are impossible. What is true is that there are sharply inclined lines which you can use to tell you the pace of trend.

When you are looking at trendlines, it is possible to spot an acceleration or deceleration of trend. While the trendline doesn't actually reflect these shifts directly, you can confirm this increase or decrease in pace by the way the overall price action looks.

When looking at price action, in this case, you'll find the curve that is traced as part of the price action chart suddenly jumps up or falls down. In this case, you can quickly spot the potential acceleration or deceleration point. When you compare that to the trendline, you'll be able to determine if there is a change in pace.

Another indicator that you can use to confirm your visual appreciation is trading volume. You can quickly spot trading volume through a combination of another line graph or a histogram. A histogram is a bar chart that plots the number of transactions completed over certain intervals. For instance, the histogram chart can plot these changes on an hourly basis. These spikes in trading volume should coincide with the spikes in price action.

One very interesting aspect of trading volume is that you will find it to be repetitive. This means that there are certain times of day or certain days in the month where action tends to pick up. These increments in trading volume are generally associated with specific events like the weekend, payday, after working hours, and so on.

Graphical Analysis

Crypto investors who do not take advantage of graphical analytics tools are doomed to suffer from bad trades. The reason for using graphical analysis tools lies in the fact that you cannot accurately detect price movements without some sort of analytical tool that can help you spot patterns.

Now, it should be noted that you don't have to live and die by charts alone. There are other factors that are involved in determining the valuation. For instance, there are psychological factors that affect investors' decisions. Nevertheless, these elements are always reflected in price. If an event is noteworthy, it will eventually be reflected in price action.

What does this mean?

It means that using charts to your advantage is essential in getting a head start on the market. The best graphical analysis tools allow you to run simulations on future behavior based on current information. These tools, while hardly perfect, give you a pretty accurate picture of what you can expect down the road, given the patterns seen at the moment.

These tools are great, especially when you are dealing with a crypto that's trading in a band. This high level of predictability makes it quite easy for you to make a profit even if it's not mind-blowing. Furthermore, you can plan ahead without having to second-guess yourself.

Additionally, graphical analysis allows you to conduct "backtesting." Backtesting refers to testing your models and assumptions on prior data. This is great because it allows you to see if your trade setups would have worked previously. As such, you can see if the price action for that specific coin will reinforce your assumptions. If you are proven wrong, then you can tweak your setup to reflect the real data.

It should be noted that backtesting and forecasting work when there isn't a high degree of volatility. Volatility means that there are significant swings in price action in a short timeframe. Generally speaking, high volatility is the result of increased trading activity, especially when investors are rushing to enter the market or looking to dump their positions. As such, you'll see wild upswings or downturns in price action.

If you are seriously looking to become a successful investor, then making the most of graphical analysis tools will enable you to make some serious gains without having to bet the farm on a hunch.

Reversal Pattern

All successful investors become adept at spotting when trend is about to reverse. This means spotting when a downward trend will switch to an upward one and vice-versa. Learning to spot trend reversal is quite useful when it comes to maximizing profit.

The underlying principle here is to buy at the lowest point and sell at the highest.

This works very well when you are in a predictable pattern, such as when a coin is trading in a range or band. So, the challenge then becomes identifying when the reversal will actually take place.

Let's consider this situation.

You are tracking the price of coin BTF. This coin is currently trading at a support level of $1.05 and a resistance level of $1.15. This means that there is a 10-cent spread among levels. Theoretically, you could get in at $1.06 and still make money. However, this is not the optimal entry point, as you could have gotten in lower. Consequently, you could have maximized your gain had you gotten in at a lower point.

By the same token, you could exit the trade at $1.09 and still make money. Again, this is not the optimal exit point, as you could have made more profit by leaving at a higher point. This is why the challenge is to spot the lowest entry point and the highest exit point. This is how you can maximize your profit.

Of course, it is virtually impossible to get in at the lower mathematical point. Also, it's quite difficult to exit at the precise moment the highest price point is hit. Unless you are dealing with a coin that is trading in a very predictable band for a long time period, this can be quite tough to determine. Nevertheless, you can still get in at a very favorable point while leaving at a highly profitable one.

So, let's look at how you can accurately spot these reversal points given a data set on a price action chart.

First, take any coin you wish to study. Generate a price action chart that is about 24 hours old. It's best not to use current information as this may change rapidly. So, using charts that are 24 to 48 hours old can be a good place to start.

Then, generate the trendline. Make sure it overlaps on the actual price action curve. This will allow you to intersect the various points in the chart with the trendline itself. Also, ensure that the trendline shows a clear bullish or bearish trend. If you have a sideways trendline, you might be better off going back further in time or just looking at another coin.

Next, take a good look at the points in which the trendline intersects with the support and resistance level. The rule of thumb is the following:

When you have a bearish trendline, that is a downward trendline, the point in which this line touches the support level will indicate the point at which a reversal to a bullish trend will take place. Likewise, a bullish trendline that intersects with the exact point of a resistance level would signal the reversal in trend to a bearish one.

This is how you can determine the entry and exit points of a trade, particularly when you are dealing with a coin that's trading in a band. As such, you can make some easy profits in such situations.

Lastly, backtest your strategy several times over using different timeframes. If you find that there is a predictable pattern repeating over and over, you could have a good option that you can trade on a regular basis. However, if you spot that your pattern doesn't hold up very well over time, then you would need to pay close attention to the signals that would indicate the reversals you need in order to enter and exit a trade.

Head and Shoulders Pattern

The head and shoulders pattern is a standard of technical analysis. This pattern is generally used to identify a potential reversal in a bearish or bullish trend. As such, it can be used to track changes in the overall trend of a given data set.

This pattern is characterized by a price action curve that has three distinct spikes. These spikes are what serve to create the head and shoulders pattern. As such, you have one peak (the first shoulder), then a larger spike (the head), followed by a third, smaller peak (the second shoulder). When this pattern emerges, you'll quickly see the reverse in trend.

Let's consider the following example:

The overall price action has been on the positive side. This has been evidenced by the price action hitting the resistance level multiple times. Then, there is a sharp spike that broke out of the resistance level before returning back down to its average. The next spike hit the resistance level and moved back down.

While this may appear to be bullish, the trendline indicates there is a downward trend. As a result, you can expect there to be a reversal in the overall trend. The reversal will be evident by a breakthrough in the support level. This means that the price will fall through the floor once the price action curve hits bottom. From there, it is uncertain how far the price will fall.

Generally speaking, following a breakthrough, the new floor is seen after the price bounces back up and then hits the same point on the floor. If you see two or three consecutive hits around the same point on the floor, then you can be relatively certain a new floor has been established. It could be that there is a new band in place, or you may expect another reversal.

In this example, the exact point in a reversal is evidenced by a succession of long candlesticks right before hitting the floor. Then, there will be one very short candlestick following the long ones. When you see this short candlestick, the reversal is about to take place.

This is the point where you can anticipate the reversal coming. If you are looking to enter a trade, this is not the best time to do it. You may end up seeing a huge drop in price before seeing a significant rebound. As such, you may have to hold on for a while before recouping your position.

The opposite case is the exact inversion. This is where you have troughs instead of peaks highlighted by a bullish trendline. This means that the price action has been low, but looks to rebound and look for a breakout.

In this case, you have a short trough punching down on the floor, then a breakthrough, followed by another punch on the floor. Just like the previous case, the reversal will come when you see a succession of long candlesticks followed by a very short one. At that point, the reversal will mean a breakout past the previous high. Now, how high the breakout will go is uncertain. You can look at previous history to get an idea of where the price may land.

It should be noted that head and shoulders with a bearish trendline needs to have clearly defined resistance levels. However, it is not required to have a clearly defined support level. By the same token, the head and shoulders pattern with a bullish trendline needs to have a clearly defined floor but not necessarily a clearly defined ceiling.

Ultimately, it's up to you to decide how low or how high you think the price action will go. When you anticipate a breakthrough, you can get in at the very low end of the trough. If you anticipate a breakout, you can sell at the highest possible point you have determined. However, a good rule of thumb is to play it conservatively. That way, you won't hold on for too long, thereby risking your profit margin.

Triple Top and Triple Bottom

The pattern known as "triple top" or "triple bottom" can serve one of two purposes.

The first is to confirm a support or resistance level. When there is a high degree of volatility or a reversal in trend, you need to find some sort of indication that there is a new support or resistance level emerging. Until you can get this confirmation, you can't be entirely sure about where the price action will ultimately land.

This is where you can use this pattern to establish if there is, in fact, a support or resistance level.

Let's consider triple tops. Following a reversal in trend from bearish to bullish, you want to establish if there is a new resistance level in place. So, you observe the peaks to find that three consecutive hits have been identified at, or close to, the same point. This can be taken as an indication of a resistance level. However, official confirmation cannot be made until you look at the candlesticks. When you look at the candlesticks, you can see a series of at least three candlesticks of roughly the same size. Then, as the price action curve begins to descend, you have a good idea of what the new resistance level looks like. As long as the trendline remains bullish or begins to level off, you can be sure that you are in a new range with a clearly defined resistance level.

In the opposite case, there are three successive bottoms following a trend reversal. As long as the same conditions apply, you can infer there is a new support level in place. This can help you determine solid entry points.

The second purpose is to spot a breakout or breakthrough. When you see three successive tops with a sharp trendline, you might be gearing up for a breakout. To get more confirmation on this, look at the trading volume. If the volume has been lower than usual, then you can expect pressure to build. Once the trading volume takes off, you can expect the breakout to take place.

The same goes for triple bottoms. When the trading volume seems to be on pause, the three successive bottoms may give you an indication that investors are only waiting for a signal to begin selling. As such, you need to pay close attention to when the trading volume picks up again. When this occurs, the price may breakthrough giving you an opportunity to pick up some good bargains.

On the whole, this pattern is rather easy to spot. The three consecutive peaks or troughs ought to provide you with enough forewarning of the break in the previous significant level. By paying attention to the triple top or bottom, trendline, and trading volume, you have all of the technical analysis indicators you need to really make sense of the price action you are seeing.

As you become more and more experienced in trading, you will be able to recognize these patterns more easily. As a result, you'll be able to make significant gains even when others may be afraid to enter the market.

CHAPTER 7

Risk Management

Risk is an inherent part of investing. Any time you choose to invest in anything, stocks, bonds, FOREX, commodities, and crypto, there is risk that is associated with it. You cannot escape it. It's there, and you need to address it accordingly. If you believe that risk is something you can skirt around, you'll be disappointed to find it biting you at some point down the road.

On the whole, risk is a question of things not working out the way you had planned. This means that you need to deal with the fact that things may not go your way at any given point in time. As such, managing risk becomes a question of figuring out what to do with it. Since you can't escape it, then the only thing you are left with is trying to understand how you can minimize its potential impact on your investment portfolio.

This is why the term "risk management" boils down to taking preventive measures that you can use to reduce the likelihood of being negatively impacted by unforeseen occurrences. These occurrences can range from mistakes in your trade setup to the so-called "black swans" that is, totally unexpected events that can cause a severe impact on your trading.

In this chapter, we are going to take a look at risk management and how it pertains to cryptocurrencies. On the whole, you'll see how risk management is a question of minimizing risk by making sound investment decisions. Therefore, we're not talking about a magic shield that will keep you safe and sound. We're talking about sound investment practices which will keep negative consequently at bay.

The Role of Brokers

Brokers are licensed professionals who are trained in money management. These individuals are trained to make investment decisions on behalf of their clients. As such, they are legally bound to make the best decisions they can be based on the information that they have available. However, please keep in mind that brokers are really only looking out for themselves. What they are really after is building their bonus. This means that they don't actually care about *you* making money; they only care about making money for themselves.

Now, in terms of risk management, you can hire a professional broker to manage your investments. In doing so, you are reducing your risk as you are handing over your investment decisions to someone who is fully invested in the trading world. In the end, all you get is a statement and a check for your earnings. But, is this truly the best you can do?

Sure, you cut risk down by trusting someone who is trained and experienced in the world of investing. But that comes at a price. In addition to the commission that you must pay to your broker, you are also on the hook for taxes and account fees. In the end, your potential earnings are whittled down by the large amount of commissions and fees you need to pay.

Needless to say, this is not the wisest investment decision you can make. As such, you are handing your money over to someone else so that they can use it to pad their own pockets. Meanwhile, you'll be lucky if you get a check large enough to fill your car's tank.

Now, if after reading this book so far you feel that simply hiring an investment professional would make life easier for you despite all the fees, then so be it. Perhaps you feel you may not have enough time to dedicate to the rigors of trading crypto. Perhaps you feel that it's just easier to pay the fees as that would save you a ton of work.

If you have an investment capital large enough, it will probably make sense. We're talking about hundreds of thousands of dollars, if not millions. However, if you are a retail investor looking to build your own path, then handing over your hard-earned cash to a broker doesn't make sense.

In addition, if you choose to invest in an ETF or a mutual fund, then you are better off simply putting your money under the mattress. These vehicles, while generally safe, deliver highly underwhelming returns. In particular, mutual funds are indexed to the stock market. As a result, they are dependent on the overall conditions of the market. If the market is down, you'll take a pounding. If the market is rocking and rolling, then you'll make money.

That doesn't sound like the best investment strategy you could make.

So, if you are ready to cut out the middleman and make some real money, then read on.

No Brokers for Crypto

There are no brokers, no funds, no middlemen when it comes to crypto. It's you and your money. This means that you have the means to make your own destiny in this market. Sure, there have been some so-called crypto ETFs popping up in various investment companies. However, they offer very underwhelming returns. These are not the type of returns you seek to make.

When you engage in the world of crypto trading, you will find that the money you make is yours. In some instances, you won't even be liable for taxes. Although, it's always best to check in your state to make sure that you have the right information as you may be on the hook for some tax payments.

Since there are no middlemen, you stand to make some good money as there are no fees and commissions to be paid. Now, it should be noted that the exchange on which you trade your coins may charge you a fee per trade. This fee is tied to the number of trades you make. So, if you make zero trades, you don't have to pay anything. However, if you make a billion trades, then you would have to fork over the corresponding sum.

In the greater scheme of things, paying a fee per trade is much better than paying a fee, commission, and account management dues. That just doesn't make sense. Plus, why would you have your money invested in stocks, especially when the market isn't in the best possible shape? When you really think about it, investing in cryptos makes a lot more sense, especially when you are looking to avoid much of the drama that comes with traditional investing.

Now, there is one catch to the crypto market. Since it doesn't have nearly as much regulation as the traditional stock market or FOREX, you need to be sure you are dealing with trustworthy sources. This means that if there is any kind of dispute regarding transactions, you are pretty much on your own. That is why you need to make sure that you know who you are dealing with.

Beyond that, the crypto space can be a wide-open field for you to make some serious returns. In addition, cryptos give you the opportunity to take control of your investment decisions. This is a powerful aspect for the average investor. By taking control of your investment portfolio, you can make the best possible decisions based on your objectives and expectations.

Cryptocurrency Wallet

Cryptos are stored in a digital wallet or vault. This is important to note. These are just files which you can store on your computer. Of course, you could if you wanted to. However, there is always the case of risk to consider. Therefore, using a digital wallet that is offered by a reputable provider makes the most sense.

As mentioned earlier, cryptos are nothing more than a sequence of computer code. That sequence is used to conduct the transactions for which it was designed. As a result, it is not the wisest idea to simply store it as a regular file on your computer. This implies that you need to find a good way of storing it securely.

Crypto exchanges like Coinbase offer a digital vault service. They don't charge you anything for storing your coins. After all, they gain by keeping the stash in the house. In a manner of speaking, it's like a regular bank that doesn't necessarily need to have cash on hand to cover all of their customers' deposits. After all, the likelihood of all customers wanting their money at the same time is rather slim.

The same goes for crypto vaults.

So, a vault service such as the one provided by Coinbase can be a good alternative for savvy investors. This reduces the amount of exposure your coins have to would-be thieves. Plus, all you need is a password to access your wallet.

Speaking of passwords, it's important for you to make sure that you make provisions for your password to be transferred to your heirs in case of your passing. If you happen to pass on unexpectedly, your heirs may never be able to access your coins. In fact, the exchange wouldn't even be able to access them as they don't have the authorization to access your coins. Hence, it's a good idea to make these kinds of provisions well in advanced.

Wallet Security

The biggest recommendation that is generally made regarding wallet security is safeguarding your password. Passwords used to access digital wallets tend to be highly complex in order to prevent thieves from getting their greedy paws on your coins. As such, it's always best to make sure your password isn't easy to crack.

When you go about opening an account for your digital tokens, finding a reputable company is always the best choice. Even if you need to pay an extra bit of cash to keep your coins safe, in the end, it's totally worth it. You can't expect to safeguard your coins by having the cheapest service in the market. In fact, when it comes to digital wallets, you get what you pay for. This means that finding the right balance between cost and security is fundamental.

The consensus best overall wallet is Coinbase. We have mentioned this company several times throughout this book since it is considered to be the best in the industry. Since Coinbase also functions as an exchange, you can purchase your coins and store them directly. Plus, you don't have to pay a dime for the wallet itself. This is an added bonus.

Other wallet companies include Trezor, Ledger, SoFi, Robinhood, Edge, and Exodus. These are all reputable companies though it's important to make sure that you do your homework on hacks and attacks that might have been made to any of these companies. Please keep in mind that thieves are always looking for vulnerabilities. So, it's always a good idea to do an online search to see just how reliable they have been. For instance, Robinhood was famously hacked some time ago. Although the company denied any customers' wallets being affected, it just goes to show that any company can be the subject of an attack at any time. This is why we strongly recommend that you double-check with companies before engaging with them.

Wallet Hacks

In theory, you could build your own digital wallet and use your computer as a storage device. However, any time your computer goes online, you are technically vulnerable to an attack. Therefore, your computer, as such, is not the best place to store any of your tokens.

One solution that some investors have found is to store their coins on an external hard drive. Since this hard drive is offline, would-be thieves have no access to it. Therefore, you can be safe that no one is going to try and steal your coins.

However, there is one catch. If you choose to store your coins in this manner, you wouldn't be able to access them readily. Thus, you need to make sure that you can access your coins rather easily, especially if you are looking to buy and sell on a regular basis. Now, if you are planning on purchasing them and simply holding on to them, then storing them in an offline device would make sense.

With that in mind, the biggest attack of your digital wallet would be through the use of malware intended to steal your password. You can download this type of malware from any number of places. Hence, having a good firewall program also comes in handy.

On the whole, your digital wallet can be hacked if you are not careful with your password. Beyond that, the only other way that your wallet could be hacked is if the vault company is hacked. While this is entirely possible (as the Robinhood case), these companies need to ensure their customers' safety.

To put the biggest heists into perspective, here is a choice list of the biggest digital wallet hacks know to date. First, Bithumb was taken for $30M worth of coins. Also, Coinrail was hit for $37.2, BitGrail $195M, and Coincheck was knocked around for $534M. This is nothing to sneeze at, to say the least. These hacks have been perpetrated by notorious international hackers. And while the companies vowed to restore their customers' coins, the loss in market value is indeed massive.

Exchange Hacks

Just like wallet hacks, exchanges are also the target of cybercriminals looking to make some easy money. When it comes to hacking an exchange, the main objective here is to hijack coin or divert coin in a transaction while avoiding the corresponding payment.

This is where the fraud takes place.

Hackers just want the coin. They could care less about making the payment that is due on the value of the coin. So, they can pose as real investors. In that regard, real investors engage in the trade unbeknownst of the true intentions behind the fraudster. The transaction takes place as the coins change hands, but the counterpart of the transaction does not. So, the investor is defrauded as they do not receive the corresponding payment. Then, the fraudsters disappear with the coin.

A lot of times, hackers will gain illegal access to an existing user's accounts. So, it's not like they can just long on the system as a brand-new user. In fact, hackers circle the internet like sharks hoping to find an unsuspecting victim. When they do, they can steal their login credentials.

This is why coin exchanges take precautions to ensure that they aren't being taken to the cleaners by cybercriminals. This also provides users the assurance that the transactions they are conducting are legit and not subject to the risk of being hacked by criminals.

Preventing Hacks

As a regular user, preventing a hack is really a matter of safeguarding your information. This generally means not sharing any kind of personal information online while also protecting the most valuable part of your account, that is, your password.

One of the most common ways that hackers like to gain access to personal information is through a scheme known as "phishing." In phishing, hackers literally cast a wide net by sending out mass emails, pretending to be a legitimate company that does business with its customers.

When customers receive "official" emails from the coin exchange, they either share the information that is requested in the email or click on the links provided in the email. This prompts the user to follow the hacker's website. Now, the hackers don't actually store any of the information on the site itself. All the page does is track keystrokes. That's how they steal your username and password. Then, they use that to go on the real site and perpetrate the crime.

Another way in which hackers gain access is through the use of malware. This generally happens when you install a virus on your computer. The virus logs keystrokes, thus causing you to unknowingly share your information with the hackers. Then, they log into your account and use it to defraud the exchange.

To prevent something like this from happening, it's important to always be suspicious of any emails that come from the exchange or any type of communication that simulates the exchange. If you are prompted to change your password by email, this is a red flag. When you are prompted to change your password because it has expired, this will happen when you actually log on to the site.

Another way in which you can prevent your information from being stolen is to avoid logging into your account(s) while you are on a public WiFi network. In this "hotpots," hackers can set up a system to intercept the flow of data traffic. As a result, they can catch information such as passwords and usernames, along with credit card information, social security numbers, and so on.

Also, if there are multiple individuals using one computer, it's best to avoid using it for your account management. By entering your information on a shared computer, you are creating an unnecessary vulnerability. This is why it's always a good idea to conduct your business on a computer that you know is completely safe.

Lastly, there is your phone. If you are planning on using your phone, even just to check your account, make sure you set up some kind of authentication. This could be something like fingerprint or face recognition ID. This could save your accounts in case your phone is lost or stolen. Many times, unscrupulous individuals steal phones, not for the phone itself, but for the information they can access. If you have a fingerprint or face ID enabled function, it is impossible for hackers to gain. They would have to literally destroy the phone in the attempt to bypass these security features.

As you can see, playing it safe goes a long way when it comes to protecting your account and data. So, do make a habit of adopting preventive measures. It can save your account while protecting the users on exchanges. This will allow you to have a great experience trading crypto while ensuring the market remains safe. All you need is some rather basic security habits. Ultimately, you have control of your accounts and your coins.

CHAPTER 8

Fundamental Computer Analysis

In this chapter, we are going to be looking at the ways in which you can utilize technical analysis tools and techniques to identify price action and thereby set up your trades effectively. So, please don't let the name throw you off. We're not going to be focusing on coding or programming. We're going to be focusing on data analysis methods. This will enable you to further develop your skills and understand with regard to trading cryptos.

The term "computer analysis" refers to the fact that we are using software tools to analyze the quantitative data generated by the price action of the coins you are tracking. This is important to note as we are not going to be crunching the numbers by hand. Of course, you could totally do it if you wanted to, but it's much better if you decided to use computer software programs to manage these data.

Also, it's important to consider that the volume of data you are going to be looking at is quite extensive. So, it would be quite time-consuming to run through the data without using computer-aided tools. This makes it imperative for you to take full advantage of the tools you have at your disposal. If you are unfamiliar with some of these tools, please take the time to go over them so that you can feel comfortable utilizing them.

Indicators for Coin Analysis

Throughout this book, we have discussed a number of indicators. These indicators can be used to help you make an assessment of the conditions surrounding the valuation of the coin itself. When you go about analyzing the overall conditions referring to the valuation of a coin, there are a number of issues that you need to take into account. So, we'll briefly go over some of the items we have already discussed while considering additional elements.

1. **Price**. Price is the most common indicator. This is the clearest indicator regarding the valuation of a coin. When you look at price, you see what the market thinks the valuation of the coin should be. Now, there are two things to consider here. First, if there is a large supply of a coin, then the price would tend to be lower. The other factor is investor perception regarding the potential of a

coin. This is a highly subjective assessment with regard to the potential demand for the coin.

2. **Trend**. We have discussed trend quite extensively. So, it's worth mentioning at this point that if the trend surrounding a crypto is predominantly bullish, then you can infer that the valuation of a currency will increase over time.

3. **Average**. When considering average, it's important to see how average prices play over a given time period. If you choose to plot a chart using only average prices, you can get a good idea of what the overall price action is like. This is where you can use the moving average indicator to make an assessment regarding the overall price action. Furthermore, charts displaying candlesticks will help you get a good sense of the opening and closing price throughout a given period.

4. **Trading volume**. Trading volume is a highly useful indicator that can help you to assess the overall amount of transactions during a given period. This is the reflection of the "popularity" of a coin. Those coins which have a higher trading volume reflect greater interest on the part of investors.

5. **Cross rates**. This is a term borrowed from FOREX. A Cross rate refers to the valuation of a coin based on different currencies or other cryptos. For example, Bitcoin is valued in US Dollars, Euros, or other cryptos like Litecoin or Ethereum. When you compare the various cross rates, you can make an assessment

according to the overall valuation of a coin. If you find that the price of Bitcoin is much higher in Litecoin than Ethereum, it could be that Litecoin is undervalued. This would reveal a lot more about Litecoin that it does about Bitcoin.

Please bear in mind that the crypto space hasn't been around for quite as long as other markets. So, this implies that the number of indicators available isn't quite as broad as other markets. This is a sign of maturity. When you have markets that have been around for a while, you will find that there are a larger number of indicators available. This is a reflection of how investors and analysts develop their own indicators to help make a better assessment. Consequently, you can expect the scope of indicators available in the crypto space will grow over time.

Ichimoku Cloud

The Ichimoku Cloud is a technical analysis tool that compares various measures at once. It is used to show support and resistance levels based on available data sets. It is intended to provide further insight into price action information beyond the traditional candlestick chart or trendline analysis. As such, this chart groups a number of indicators so that their analysis in unison provides a greater data set. The cross-referencing of the various data points enables investors and analysts to make more informed decisions into entry and exit points.

This tool can be used with stocks, FOREX, and commodities. Therefore, it is perfectly applicable to the world of crypto. All you need is the corresponding data to make the set work. These charts can be generated by the information service available on your trading platform. These charts are generated automatically by simply overlaying the various indicators in a single chart.

The basis for the Ichimoku Cloud is the traditional candlestick chart that plots price action over a given timeframe. Since the data represented on the candlestick chart itself is rather limited, the Ichimoku Cloud looks to augment this information. Thus, moving average indicators are used to supplement the information contained in this chart. Consequently, the 26-period and the 52-period moving average are overlaid.

When you hear the term "26-period" moving average, the word "period" refers to the specific time periods analyzed as part of the chart. Generally speaking, a period in this sense of the word refers to hours. Of course, the period could be longer, depending on the type of asset you are analyzing. For example, stocks use the 20-day moving average. This means that price action is tracked over days and not hours. However, the FOREX market, which is much more dynamic than stocks, uses hourly periods to track price action. As such, you are looking at a timeframe of about 24 to 48 hours, meaning roughly two days of action.

There are five parts that need to be calculated to make the Ichimoku Cloud:

- Conversion line
- Base line

- Leading Span A

- Leading Span B

- Lagging Span

These elements are what create the cloud in the graph. When you trace the cloud, you end up getting the predictive measure of what you can expect down the road. As such, the Ichimoku Cloud is quite good at enabling you to predict future support and resistance levels based on available information. Plus, you can spot where potential reversals may occur.

In its calculation, you are essentially taking the high and low prices of the 26-periods. This enables you to calculate the leading span, which seeks to determine price action 26 periods into the future. The leading span A is based on the high while leading span B is based on the low price. Once you have this setup, you will see a green cloud and a red one. The green cloud indicates prices above the average while the red cloud indicates prices below the average.

On its own, the Ichimoku Cloud is generally used as a means of confirming resistance and support levels. Consequently, you can pair this indicator with a simple overlay of the moving average along with other technical analysis indicators such as trend, trading volume, and others such as the Relative Strength Index (RSI). The RSI is used to evaluate an asset is being overbought or oversold. Thus, you can use the RSI to confirm any assumptions you may have about a coin's overall momentum. It could be that price action is reacting to an oversold condition or hasn't yet reacted to an overbought condition.

Either way, the RSI, along with other indicators, can serve to create a solid technical analysis foundation for your assessments.

The biggest drawback of the Ichimoku Cloud is that the chart is filled with a great deal of information on it. At first glance, it can be quite overwhelming. Thus, you can use charting software to hide certain lines. This allows you to analyze the entire chart in individual segments. Then, you can look at the entire action to see the interaction of all the data.

In addition, the Ichimoku Cloud is based on historical information. This means that you are taking previous price action to project into the future. While this is a perfectly valid statistical model, the fact that you are basing your predictions on a short timeframe means that you won't be able to project very far into the future. If you choose to look at longer data sets to overcome this situation, you will find that its predictive capabilities are quite limited. This is why the Ichimoku Cloud should always be paired with other indicators in order to obtain a broader picture of the price action.

Oscillators

Oscillators are used as a part of technical analysis tools to determine trend and momentum. In the world of FOREX, oscillators are quite commonly used to make a predictive analysis. Now, it should be noted that oscillators don't study trend; as such, rather they study "momentum." Momentum refers to the condition of being overbought or oversold.

When discussing the RSI, we mentioned these two conditions. The reason why they are relevant is due to the fact that trading volume will indicate if an asset is being predominantly bought or predominantly sold. This is important to take into account as either condition will generate momentum in one direction or another.

Hence, trend refers specifically to price action, while momentum refers to the trading volume, that is, the specific amount of "buy" or "sell" transactions.

On the surface, when an asset is oversold, it means that holders are getting rid of their positions. This would imply a potential fall in price. On the other hand, when an asset is being overbought, this means that investors are looking to acquire as much as they can. Therefore, you can assume that price will move up based on increased demand.

Additionally, when an asset is being oversold, you can infer that its price is overvalued. This means that holders assume that the price is higher than expected and thus would like to sell before it falls. Also, when an asset is being overbought, investors feel that it is undervalued and thus want to scoop it up before price increases.

This is why the use of oscillators helps you determine if you are dealing with a coin that is actually under or overvalued.

If you are looking to purchase, and overbought coin means that the market feels it is undervalued. As a result, you could consider getting in. By the same token, if you are holding a coin and see an oversold condition, that is an indication that it's time to liquidate your position before price plunges.

The easiest way to calculate oscillation is to take the current price and subtract it from the previous price. This simple formula implies that if you get a positive value, then momentum is increasing as price is gaining. If the result is negative, then this implies that price is falling, and momentum is negative.

The current price used in this calculation is based on the specific moment you are analyzing, for instance, at this very moment. The previous price is rather subjective. You can choose to compare price action on an hourly basis. So, if it's currently 11 am, you can subtract the 11 am price from the 10 am price. You can do this as far back as you like though the industry standard as an hour by hour basis.

Another commonly-used oscillator is known as the stochastic oscillator. The term "stochastic" is a statistical term used to refer to randomness. So, this oscillator looks to determine if there is randomness in the price action you are analyzing. This is important as randomness would be indicative of market forces outside of the traditional patterns which you may have observed. Randomness may be the result of unforeseen events that are putting pressure on the market as opposed to investor expectations and psyche.

Stochastic oscillators are used to determine buy and sell signals. This oscillator can be used in conjunction with the moving average and RSI to provide further indication of trend reversals and divergences that may occur in pricing. As such, you can use this oscillator to establish if there is a high or low degree in the randomness associated with the price action you are analyzing.

Alligators

Alligators are commonly used in the world of FOREX to determine if there are trends forming or to establish the absence of one. When a trend is under formation, the alligator can tell you which direction it is going. If there is no trend, then the alligator will confirm this.

The reason why this indicator is called an alligator has to do with the behavior of trend. So, it's not that the charting action resembles an alligator in any way. Rather, it's the behavior that resembles an alligator's behavior.

This analogy is based on the fact that an absence of trend, that is a sideways or horizontal trendline, resembles a sleeping alligator. However, there is a point in which the alligator must wake up. When the alligator wakes up, it will be hungry and in search of prey. The premise is that the longer the alligator sleeps, the hungrier it will be. This means that once the sideways trend is broken, the new trend, bearish or bullish, will be considerably sharper.

The alligator formation is composed of three separate moving averages. These are called "balance lines." When these lines are compared, you can determine if the sideways trend will be bearish or bullish. Most importantly, you can also determine how sharp it will be.

The first line is called the alligator's jaw. This is generally marked in blue, and it is composed of a 13-period moving average. It is then moved forward by an additional 8 candlesticks (21 periods in total).

The second line is called the alligator's teeth. This line is represented in red. This is the moving average of eight periods, then moved forward and an additional 5 (13 candlesticks total).

The third line is called the alligator's lips. This line is shown in green. It is the 5- period moving average and then moved 3 candlesticks forward (8 in total).

The comparison of these three lines tells you where the trend will likely end up at any given point. The absence of trend can be spotted when the three lines are very closed bunched up together. The closer they stick together, the greater the absence of trend. The alligator wakes up when the green line crosses over the other two. Since the green line is the fastest moving average, it indicates the momentum of trend formation. If its spike is noticeably sharper than the other two, then this indicates the level of hunger in the alligator. As such, the divergence of the green line in comparison with the other two indicates how pronounced the new trend will be.

Perhaps the most difficult aspect of the alligator pattern is to identify the exact moment when the break in horizontal trend will happen. So, it's a matter of keeping a close eye on

108

potential crossovers. This is the clearest indicator of when the break in sideways trend will actually occur.

Japanese Candlestick Patterns

In this pattern, we are going to be looking exclusively at candlesticks and the patterns they represent. Consequently, we will be discussing how you can read candlesticks effectively as part of your overall research task.

It should be noted that we are going to use a simple candlestick chart. As such, we are not going to be using any other statistical indicators beyond candlesticks. However, you might think they are simply candlesticks; what they reveal is far more telling.

Please bear in mind that a candlestick measures the following: the high price, the low price, and the spread among the opening and closing price. As such, the candlestick's body represents the spread between the opening and closing price with the upper line represents the high price, and the lower line represents the low price. Additionally, when the body of the stick is black, it indicates that the closing price was lower than the opening. When the stick is white (or transparent), it indicates that the closing price was higher than the opening.

This is where the various Japanese interpretations of the candlesticks come into play. They represent the various ways in which the sticks can tell you what to expect from the information seen in the chart. This can help you to figure out where the momentum is going at any given time.

The Spinning Top

The first configuration to look at is called a "spinning top." This configuration is highlighted by a narrow (or short) candlestick body. The color is essentially meaningless, while the high and low price are exactly the same (or very close to being exactly the same). This configuration indicates a high degree of indecision among investors. Essentially, it means that there were no "winners" or "losers" in that period; everyone broke even, so to speak.

There are two possible interpretations of a spinning top. If there is a spinning top during an upward trend, it could signal that there aren't that many buyers left. This is a signal for a potential reversal to a downward trend. On the other hand, if a spinning top is present in a downward trend, it indicates that there aren't that many sellers left in the market. As such, it signals a potential reversal to an upward trend.

The Marubozu Candlestick

The "Marubozu" stick (which literally means "bald" in Japanese) indicates the stick has no "shadow." This means that the upper and lower lines are non-existent. What that means is that the high and low price are exactly the same.

There are two types of Marubozu. A white Marubozu means that the opening price equals the low price, and the close price equals the price. Consequently, the stick is white, but the shadows are gone. In contrast, a black Marubozu means that the opening price equals the high price and the closing price is the same as the low price. Therefore, you can interpret that the asset lost in value.

Here are the possible interpretations of a Marubozu:

The emergence of a white Marubozu at the end of an upward trend signals that a continuation of the trend is likely. If you spot a white Marubozu at the end of a downward trend, then a reversal is likely.

The emergence of a black Marubozu at the end of a downward trend means the trend is likely to continue. If you see a black Marubozu at the end of an upward trend, then a reversal is likely to happen.

The Marubozu candlesticks are great at spotting potential trend reversals or continuations, particularly if you are following resistance levels and trendlines. If you spot these sticks at points in which resistance and support levels are going to intersect with a trendline, then you definitely have the confirmation you need to make your assessments accurately.

The Doji Candlesticks

Doji candlesticks are used to measure the struggle between buyers and sellers. In essence, you are looking at the turf war that may emerge between the two as the jockey for position in a market. The Doji can also represent indecision, especially when there is a great deal of uncertainty surrounding a market.

The easiest way to identify a Doji candlestick is by the very narrow body. So, you have the upper and lower shadows with a very thin body that basically resembles a straight line. This means that neither buyers nor sellers were able to really make any kind of headway during that particular time. If you happen to spot these sticks, then you are in for one of four possible configurations.

1. **Long-legged Doji**. This is akin to a perfectly centered cross. The upper and lower shadows are the same length, while a very narrow body slices both lines right through the middle. This indicates a high degree of indecision as neither buyers nor sellers were able to come out ahead.

2. **Dragonfly Doji**. This candlestick has practically no upper shadow with the narrow body all the way to the top while a very long lower body is visible. This configuration is generally seen at the point of a possible reversal as the asset's open, close and high prices are the same. The trend reversal could go either way, so it is neither bearish nor bullish.

3. **Gravestone Doji**. This configuration is the opposite of the Dragonfly. This stick has a long upper shadow while the lower shadow is quite short. The narrow body

is located at the bottom of the stick. This is generally a bearish sign that indicates a potential reversal. In this stick, the open, close, and low price are all the same.

4. **Four price Doji.** In this stick, all four prices open, close, high, and low are exactly the same, or very close to it. Therefore, the stick just has the narrow, horizontal body with no visible upper and lower shadow. This candlestick indicates the highest possible level of indecision in the market. It is generally seen at the very top or very bottom of a trend. It is usually the confirmation of the uppermost or lowermost point. Thus, the next stick would indicate the official beginning of the new trend.

When you are dealing with Doji, you need to be certain about the preceding sticks. This will serve to understand where trend is heading and where you can expect it to move going forward. Consequently, these sticks cannot be interpreted in isolation. They need to be seen within the context of the entire time period you are analyzing.

In general, you can interpret Doji in the following manner:

If you see a Doji following a series of black Marobozu, then the Doji indicates that sellers are beginning to grow tired. This means that there are fewer and fewer sellers. In order for the falling price to continue, more sellers would be needed in the market. But since sellers are basically exhausted, buyers will soon flood the market, triggering a reversal in trend. The confirmation of the trend reversal would be a white Marubozu. This would be a great time to buy.

The opposite scenario is also true. If you spot a Doji following a series of white Marubozu, then what you have is a series of buyers become exhausted. This means that the number of investors interested in purchasing is becoming lower. Therefore, the Doji would indicate the point in which asset holders are ready to begin selling. This would mean falling prices as the market becomes flooded with supply. This would be the ideal time to sell. The confirmation of the new trend would be represented by a black Marubozu. If you haven't already liquidated your position by then, you should consider selling before your profits begin to shrink.

Japanese sticks are not to be taken as the sole indicator of a reversal or continuation of trend. If you spot these in addition to the other indicators that we have outlined throughout this book, you will find a very good indication of the patterns that you seek. Therefore, you can plan your strategy accordingly. It's also important to use Japanese sticks as a means of confirming your overall assessment of price action. You will find that Japanese sticks are a great way of confirming what you have already been able to spot at plain sight.

Cryptocurrency Market Regulations

One of the biggest aspects of the crypto space is regulation. Given the fact that cryptos are rather new, there are many aspects that users and investors might be unsure about. Therefore, it's important to do some research in order to understand what regulation applies to the crypto space and how you can take advantage of it.

In this section, we are going to look at how the crypto market is regulated, or unregulated, and how you can use that to your advantage. As a disclaimer, please ensure that you get any legal advice from a licensed professional. In this manner, you can avoid committing any illegal action inadvertently. The last thing that we want is for you to accidentally engage in any activity that might be construed as illegal. Thus, always make sure that you seek the proper legal counsel whenever you are in doubt.

Crypto Regulation

Crypto regulation is scant at best. Only a handful of countries around the world have specific regulations regarding cryptocurrencies. This basically means that cryptos are not illegal, but it also means they aren't legal, either.

One of the aspects which are perfectly clear is that no country recognizes any crypto as legal tender. This means that cryptos may be used to settle private accounts among individuals. However, the use of cryptos does not constitute a legally binding agreement. In a manner of speaking, it's like swapping goods. This would not constitute a legal purchase as money legal tender was exchanged. Therefore, the seller cannot claim any benefit from the sale, while the buyer cannot claim they were defrauded in any way.

Perhaps the biggest concern when it comes to regulation in the crypto market is the issue of paying taxes. Depending on the country where you live, you might be on the hook for taxes based on the gains you make. Now, it should be noted that very few countries tax cryptos as assets. For instance, Israel considers cryptos to be assets. As such, holders are liable to pay taxes on them. Similarly, Bulgaria taxes cryptos as assets. This means that holders would pay a tax similar to what homeowners pay their property.

In other countries, profits made on the trade of cryptos are taxed. For instance, Argentina and Spain tax cryptos as part of an individual's income tax. Switzerland taxes cryptos as they would foreign currency. In the UK, individuals pay capital gains tax on any profits made from trading cryptos.

As you can see, the various ways in which countries regulate cryptos for fiscal purposes is rather broad. In the United States, cryptos are not subject to any taxation. However, the gains made from the trading of cryptos are. So, it's always best to double-check with your local state for any sales tax on cryptos while it's also important to double-check any applicable federal taxes that might be applicable. At the time of writing, crypto traders are only subject to capital gains tax. This means that making money on cryptos is taxed much in the same way the gains on the sale of a house would be.

Crypto Deregulation

It should be noted that the lack of regulation within the crypto space is actually an advantage when you consider the vast amount of regulation in the stock and commodities markets. Therefore, trading cryptos is largely up to the individuals who engage in trading them.

In essence, if you bought a bunch of coins, you are basically up to whatever the market dictates them t be worth. In a manner of speaking, it's like buying a car. The government cannot regulate what a car is worth. This is entirely up to the market.

Detractors of the crypto market claim that the lack of government oversight makes it inherently dangerous to trade in this space. They claim that there are no consumer protections in place. Therefore, if you happen to get fleeced or defrauded in a deal, there is nothing you can do. While criminal charges may apply as far as the scam itself, there is nothing that can regulate the trade of cryptos themselves.

On the other hand, supporters of the crypto space highlight this to be one of the best aspects of cryptocurrencies. Since these are meant to be decentralized, there is a clear intent to ensure that there is little government interference.

While it is true that having legal backing makes transactions safer and easier to manage, it should also be noted that too much government interference tends to make markets rather inefficient. If you are seriously looking into the possibility of buying and selling cryptos, the best way to manage this is to ensure that you are dealing with reputable companies and individuals. Any backdoor deals are almost always a sign of trouble.

This is why any underground markets and exchanges are best avoided. And yes, it is true that there are illegal transactions conducted in cryptocurrency. This is why you want to avoid any shady characters as much as possible. It could very well be that you end up getting mixed up with the wrong crowd.

Beyond that, the crypto space offers a great deal of opportunity for up-and-coming investors. Cryptos are here to stay. So, it's a question of understanding the market and knowing where to place your chips. If done right, you can make a fortune in the crypto space. At worst, you can make modest returns that are good enough to supplement your income. Of course, it's always a good idea to keep your eye on the price. Who knows, you may get in on the next Bitcoin right from the start. That certainly sounds like something to look forward to. There is plenty of room for growth. This is just the beginning of the future.

CHAPTER 9

Cryptotrading Psychology

Investors from all walks of life have varying types of mindsets. These mindsets can be conservative or openly aggressive. While these are the extremes, so to speak, it's important to consider that you don't have to conform to a specific type of mindset in order to be successful. You just have to learn how to manage your own mindset so that you can set yourself up to be successful.

In this regard, making money in cryptotrading is a combination of technical skills and good instincts. When you combine both aspects correctly, you can develop a discipline that will set you up for success at all points throughout your trading endeavors. If you are unable to manage the psychological aspects that come with trading, then you might find yourself in a disadvantageous position.

This is why this chapter is dedicated to analyzing the mindset of a successful cryptotrader and how you can adopt the best traits. Most important, you will find that these traits do not require you to overhaul your personality. All it requires is for you to manage your mindset in such a way that you are making the right kind of choices based on the information you have available.

Best of all, you will find that being cognizant of the weaknesses in your own mindset will help develop a long-term approach that can translate into other types of investments beyond cryptos. In the end, you could be setting up what might be a long and prosperous trading career.

The Typical Cryptotrading Mindset

The "typical" mindset is to make as much money as possible. Plain and simple. This is what all investors seek. After all, no one goes into investing thinking to lose money. Thus, it's important to consider the role that expectations play.

When the average individual goes into any kind of investment (not just cryptos), they may build unrealistic expectations in their mind. They might think they are going to clean up and become rich overnight. They may even buy into the false promises made by some companies that purport easy money-making schemes.

These are the ads you really need to be careful with.

Sure, it's not hard to make money in cryptos. However, you need to know what you are doing. That's what this book is all about. Part of that knowledge and understanding is realizing that you won't become rich overnight. Of course, you could make some decent money in a short period of time. But then again, it takes time and effort to build the type of portfolio that will guarantee you a good quality of life.

This is why novice investors ought to look at this type of investment as a means of supplementing their income. In the end, this supplemental income can serve to pay bills, cut down on debt, or save up for larger expenses such as a new car or a down payment on a home.

If you believe the stories that some so-called experts use to sell their gimmicks, then it's best you gave these stories further thought. The fact is that get-rich-quick schemes deliver underwhelming results in the best of cases.

Consequently, the "typical" mindset is based on high hopes or unrealistic expectations. In fact, you'll find that some novice investors get into cryptos, FOREX, or stocks in the hopes of suddenly quitting their job and living a fancy lifestyle filled with travel and exotic quirks.

This could not be farther from the truth.

The most successful investors spend the bulk of their time studying the markets and planning their next moves. They spend a great deal of their attention, looking at how to improve their investment strategy. This is what leads them to be the successful investors that they are.

Now, we're not saying that you should give up your regular life and immerse yourself full-time into graphs and charts. What we are saying is that living a lavish lifestyle is usually the result of hard work and dedication to investing. Additionally, your goal should not be to quit your day job. Your ultimate goal should be to build up enough revenue streams so that you don't have to depend on just one source of income.

This is what true financial independence is all about.

When you don't depend on your paycheck or the gains you make trading, you can truly become free of the rat race. Once you have the ability to choose what to do with your time and your efforts, you have the ability to truly live the life that you want to live.

Now that certainly sounds like something great, doesn't it?

The fact is that what we all aspire is to become free of debt and have the luxury to take time off, travel, or just spend time with our loved ones. This is the underlying idea behind investing. It's not just about making money for the sake of making money. It's about finding what you truly want out of life.

The Successful Cryptotrading Mindset

A successful mindset boils down to your ability to manage your expectations while putting in the time and effort needed to become a successful investor. This is the main objective. Developing the skills you need to become a successful investor will enable you to grow both in terms of your knowledge as well as your experience.

With that in mind, here are some helpful tips which will allow you to develop a discipline that will ensure your success at all points of your trading career.

1. **Set a realistic target**. Firstly, think about how much money you could reasonably make at the outset of your trading career. This could be something as simple as two or three hundred dollars. Yet, understanding that at least you'd be turning a profit from the first week you are trading ought to be enough to keep you motivated. In reality, it all boils down to your investment capital. If you invest thousands per trade, you could make a good deal of money. But if you start out with a few hundred dollars, then you need to work your way up. It will take some time, but you will get there. By keeping your eyes on the prize, you'll get there very soon.

2. **Reinvest only a part of your winnings**. Some investors like to sink all of their profits back into investing. Sure, this is a great way to make your investment capital grow quickly. However, it's not always the best way to go about managing your money. This is why you should only reinvest a part of your money. The rest

of the money should go toward things that you need to pay off or even a small luxury. Even if it's just going to dinner on a Friday night, spending some of your earnings on yourself will go a long way.

3. **Set up a schedule**. While you shouldn't look at trading as if it were an obligation, it's always a good idea to set up a schedule. This builds a routine that will help you stay focused on your goals. When you trade in your "free time," you'll find that you are rather inconsistent. When this happens, it's tough to build momentum. As you build momentum through a series of successful trades, you will need to keep moving forward at a consistent pace. Otherwise, you'll let your success cool off. By the same token, if you fall into a losing streak, you have a greater chance of breaking it by being consistent as opposed to "taking time off."

4. **Don't dwell on the past.** Whether you win or lose, it's best to let go of the past. When you have a hot streak, you might get caught up in your own success. You might think that you have everything down, and there is no need for further study or research. This may lead to a false sense of security. Needless to say, it is not a good place to be. If you happen to fall into a cold streak, you might be down and upset with yourself. If you dwell on negative experiences for too long, you'll end up killing any interest you may have in investing. This is why you need to let go of the past and focus on what's coming up ahead. This is how you can truly develop laser-sharp focus.

5. **Celebrate both wins and losses.** Celebrating wins is easy. You high-five everyone and brag about your accomplishments. That's all well and fine. However, you should also celebrate defeat as each loss leaves you with a valuable lesson. If you take losses in stride, you'll end up learning so much. This is the type of knowledge you can't buy with money. It's like becoming battle-tested. No amount of courses and training can give you combat experience. As you gain that experience, you'll be able to truly focus on your life and what you have to gain.

With these insights, you will develop a strong mindset that will be impossible to break down. Over time, you will develop the skills and discipline that you need to become a successful investor. So, there is nowhere to go but up!

CHAPTER 10

Glossary Of Basic Cryptocurrency Terms

- Altcoin

This term is a combination of the words "alternative" and "coin." As such, "altcoin" refers to any cryptocurrency that is an alternative to Bitcoin. Therefore, this term includes virtually all cryptos except Bitcoin.

- ASIC

Acronym for the Australian Securities & Investment Commission. This is the government organization that oversees trading of financial assets and securities.

- Bears

"Bears" refers to a pessimistic view of the market and trends. Any time an asset loses value or the market is in a downward situation, the term "bearish" is used.

- Bitcoin

A cryptocurrency consisting of a digital token that can be used to settle accounts and facilitate commercial transactions. It is the most popular cryptocurrency and the most valuable.

- itcoin address

A digital address which serves as the destination for a payment in Bitcoin. It is an alphanumeric code consisting of 26-35 characters. It generally begins with the numbers 1, 3, or BC1. Additionally, a dedicated wallet can also serve as a destination for a payment issued in Bitcoin.

- Bitcoin cash

A spinoff crypto of the traditional Bitcoin cryptocurrency. It was launched in 2017. Since then, it has been split up into Bitcoin Cash and Bitcoin SV.

- Bitcoin Wallet

Digital repository where digital Bitcoin tokens are stored. It can be an individual vault service or an exchange such as Coinbase.

- Blockchain

Digital ledger technology on which cryptocurrencies are built upon. It is used to verify transactions and create transparency among users.

- Bulls

This term is used any time optimistic expectations are set regarding a market, asset, or individual security. When investors are optimistic about an asset, they are said to be "bullish." When trend is "bullish," it refers to increasing price action.

- Cloud Mining

Internet-based computer power used to generate a digital token of any crypto. Dedicated datacenters are used to serve as the underlying computing power for blockchain technology. In exchange, these datacenters receive a digital token, which can later be traded for a profit.

- Crowdsale

A "crowdsale" is a public online event in which participants purchase digital cryptocurrency tokens. This event is akin to an auction. Buyers and sellers meet to swap coins or cryptos for legal tender.

- Dump

A quick sale of an asset usually the result of a sudden drop in price. To "dump" an asset means to sell as soon as possible, often below the expected price. The main point is to exit a position before the price falls into red territory.

- Ethereum

An altcoin. It is a blockchain that produces a cryptocurrency called "Ether," which can be used to settle accounts and facilitate payments. It is a common alternative to Bitcoin or Litecoin.

- Farm

Process in which dedicate computing power looks to generate cryptocurrency tokens. It is also referred to as "mining." In this process, computers are dedicated to conducting the processes outlined by the specific blockchain in order to produce token. These tokens can then be resold for a profit.

- Fiat

The term used to refer to legal tender as issued by a sovereign government. The word "fiat" refers to "decree," that is, the currency derives its value from a government decree and not by any characteristics which give it value as is the case of gold.

- Fork

This term is used to refer to the action in which a crypto is split into two separate coins. This can be done to increase its supply or to dedicate part of one blockchain to a different type of process. A common example of this is the fork created from Bitcoin. Bitcoin was split up into Bitcoin Cash and Bitcoin SV. All three are separate coins though they share the same blockchain technology.

- ICO

An acronym which refers to an "initial coin offering." Some coin issuers would rather launch a set number of coins into the market as opposed to mining them. ICOs can be purchased by investors much in the same way companies issues their IPOs (initial public offering).

- Litecoin

An altcoin. Litecoin is used as an alternative to Bitcoin. It is in the same ballpark as Ethereum. It can be used to settle accounts or facilitate commercial transactions.

- Market Depth

The amount of cryptocurrency supply for a specific coin or group of coins. It also refers to the overall supply in the market.

- Masternode (Proof of Stake)

A computer, or network of computer which combines its power, used to ensure the integrity of a coin network. In essence, a masternode is a computer system that houses a crypto's full ledger history as opposed to having the ledger history split up into various computer systems.

- Miner

Person or organization dedicated to the production of cryptocurrency tokens. Also known as a "farmer."

- Mining

Process in which dedicate computing power looks to generate cryptocurrency tokens. It is also referred to as "farming." In this process, computers are dedicated to conducting the processes outlined by the specific blockchain in order to produce tokens. These tokens can then be resold for a profit.

- Network complexity

This term refers to the level of sophistication that is involved in setting up a computer network either as part of the blockchain or the digital ledger. It can also refer to the process of mining or farming for coins.

- Order

The action of placing a trade. There are two types of orders, "buy" and "sell."

- Peak

A spike in price which leads to a high point in price. A peak usually signals an increase in overall price trend.

- Pending

A transaction that has not been completed until certain conditions are met such a target price or timeframe.

- Pool

The action of "pooling" the resources of various miners in order to increase computing power, thereby enabling greater capacity for generating crypto tokens.

- PoS Mining (Proof of Stake)

The process in which individuals verify transactions on a blockchain. The Proof of Stake process validates a transaction, thereby leading to the generation of a digital token.

- Pump

The action in which the price is driven up as a result of increased demand. When price is pumped up, it can surpass previous highs.

- Satoshi

Purported pseudonym used by the creators of Bitcoin blockchain technology.

- Swing

A term referring to the fluctuations in market prices. It also refers to changes in trend as observed by reversals from bearish to bullish and so on.

- Tokens

Digital coins which make up a cryptocurrency.

- Transaction

Action in which two sides come to an agreement. There is usually an exchange of some sort. The transaction can be finalized either by the use of legal tender or a cryptocurrency.

CONCLUSION

Thank you for making it to the end of this volume. We hope that the information you found herein has been helpful in your discovery of cryptocurrencies and how you can invest in this exciting new market.

By now, you have everything you need to get started investing in cryptos. Best of all, the entire process has been rather straightforward. As such, there are no complex processes or the need for advanced college degrees.

Making money in cryptos is a combination of both savvy and perseverance. When you are able to combine these elements, you will find that making money as an investor in this field is not nearly as hard as you might have thought.

So, what's next?

Well, the time has come to get to work. Please do your homework into crypto exchange, which offers you the support you need in order to get started in this dynamic market. Most importantly, please look for an exchange which can offer you the security measures you need in order to ensure that your coins are kept nice and safe.

Given the fact that the crypto space is a rather new market, you have the opportunity to get in now, while most investors are still unfamiliar with the concept of making profits through the trade of digital tokens.

So, what are you waiting for?

Go on and get started today. When you realize just how much money you can make trading cryptos, you will regret not having gotten into it sooner.

Thanks again for taking the time to read this book. If you have found it to be useful and informative, do leave a comment so that other readers can discover the value which you have found herein. And by all means, tell your friends, family, and colleagues about this book if you feel they too will benefit from it.

Happy trading!

www.ingramcontent.com/pod-product-compliance
Lightning Source LLC
Chambersburg PA
CBHW081818200326
41597CB00023B/4303